Advance Praise for *Keeping the Covenant*

"There is simply nothing else like it! *Keeping the Covenant* is hands down the best contemporary resource for pastoral leadership in today's church. It is eminently practical, clear, and wise — and captures Thomas Sweetser's breadth of experience and depth of wisdom. I hope all who read this remarkable book will pass it on to the pastoral leaders of their parish. This book should be required reading for all seminarians, lay ecclesial ministers, and pastors."

— Donald Cozzens, author of
Faith That Dares to Speak and *Freeing Celibacy*

"*Keeping the Covenant* is grounded in a vision and overflowing with practical strategies for enfleshing it in parish life. One aspect of the vision is captured in the subtitle: taking parish to the next level. The deeper dimension is communicated through the image of the covenantal relationship between God and the parish community, a relationship made visible in the ways that ownership of the parish is shared by pastor, staff, leaders, and people. Sweetser is realistic about the varied patterns and dynamics of parishes (multiethnic, merged, of varied size), and the ways of expanding leadership. To nurture a vision, including vision of the possible, this book is an invaluable resource."

— Zeni Fox, Ph.D., Seton Hall University, author of
New Ecclesial Ministry: Lay Professionals Serving the Church

"A wonderful book! Fr. Sweetser challenges the intentional or 'successful' parish to go to a higher level. By understanding the notion of covenant, we begin to understand the sacred trust that is the parish."

— Donna L. Ciangio, O.P., Church Leadership
Consultation (from the foreword)

Keeping the Covenant

Keeping the Covenant

Taking Parish to the Next Level

THOMAS P. SWEETSER, S.J.

A Crossroad Book
The Crossroad Publishing Company
New York

Grateful thanks to my two co-workers, Sr. Peg Bishop, O.S.F., and Deb Ebratt, who have shaped the content of this book and have helped bring it to completion. Thanks, as well, to my sister, Kathleen Hage, for her careful and accurate editing, and to Jeremy Langford for finding a home for this book at the Crossroad Publishing Company.

www.CrossroadPublishing.com

Printed in the United States of America on acid-free paper

The text of this book is set in 11.5/15.5 Goudy Old Style.
The display face is Tiffany.

Library of Congress Cataloging-in-Publication Data

Sweetser, Thomas P.
    Keeping the covenant : taking parish to the next level / Thomas P. Sweetser.
       p. cm.
    Includes bibliographical references and index.
    ISBN-13: 978-0-8245-2466-1 (alk. paper)
    ISBN-10: 0-8245-2466-7 (alk. paper)
    1. Church renewal – Catholic Church. 2. Covenants – Religious aspects – Catholic Church. I. Title.
BX1746.S86 2007
253′.088282 – dc22

                                       2007022598

2   3   4   5   6   7   8   9   10   12   11   10   09

To pastors and those overseeing parishes,
who, against all odds, still manage to lead well
and invite others to join them in directing the parish.

And to all those on parish staffs
or active in parish leadership and ministry positions.
Despite many challenges and difficulties,
they remain dedicated and faithful
to the dream of the parish
reaching its full potential.

Contents

Foreword

One colleague of mine is a religious sister who serves as a part-time staff person in two parishes after having served in a diocesan office for many years. She loves the people, differences, successes, and challenges of both places. This sister recently said to me, "Parish is where it's at!" She said this with such enthusiasm, sincerity, and joy, that it made me stop and think about the nature of parish and what gives life to its people and staff.

What makes her so happy? It is that, in her case, both parishes have effective collaborative leadership among pastor, staff, councils, and lay leaders. These combined groups have the ability to create an atmosphere where Christ is present and people are called and involved in the mission.

Parish is where it's at because that's where the life of the church is. That's where we worship and celebrate Christ — where people and families come for comfort, healing, forgiveness, support, faith formation, sacraments, and the opportunity to serve. Just as the parish is critical to the life of the church, the pastor and parish life coordinator, staff, and leadership are critical to the life and development of the parish.

There is a lot of talk today about "successful" parishes. But what makes a parish successful? After working with hundreds of parishes, I have found that the keys are strong leadership, good skills, open and listening hearts, a spirit of joy and communion, and being intentional on several levels. Since, through canon law, our parish structure places a priest as the shepherd of a parish, we need to begin there. Also, in many parishes and missions in our country, religious women and men, deacons, and laity are appointed by the bishop as parish life coordinators. Since they too lead parishes where there are not enough priests, they too need to be included.

The leader must understand the call to lead a parish as a call by God to service and mission. It is not about the leader's personal spirituality or personal direction, but about the sacred role of leading others to deeper union with Christ. That understanding has to be present in all parish leaders so that the parish is not "about me" or "what I want" but about the mission of Jesus.

The pastors or parish life coordinators are the primary theologians of the church for the people of their parishes. They are the ones who weekly, and more often through personal encounter, make the connections between revelation and people's experience. They accomplish this through preaching, teaching, witness, listening, and working shoulder to shoulder in ministries. The pastors or parish life coordinators are the primary leaders of the community, the ones who call people to mission and help them find connection with the sacred, the mystery of life and faith and the sacraments. They guide the leaders and parishioners in becoming intentional and attentive in shaping the mission.

The "intentional" parish knows who and what it is. Being intentional means that parish leadership takes time to create or update a mission statement, reflect, plan, develop, and evaluate in an organized and regular fashion. Regular meetings of parish staff, parish pastoral council, finance council, and ministry leaders all contribute to the sense of direction, goals, and good ministry that a parish has. The intentional parish is about "excellent parish ministry" in the name of Jesus Christ.

Quite a number of years ago, the United States Conference of Catholic Bishops published a document entitled *A Parish: People, Mission, Structure.* It was developed out of the Parish Project, lead by Monsignor Philip Murnion, after a series of studies, consultations, and country-wide regional conferences. The conclusion was that parishes were successful when they operated intentionally in precisely those three areas: people, mission, and structure — and I find that this still holds true today.

The parish remains a complex balance of spirit and organization. For most parishioners, it is their primary way of connecting with Christ and the larger church. It is the place of prayer, sacraments, communion, and community, as well as the place that urges them to be involved publicly in the mission of Jesus Christ. A parish requires flexible yet disciplined leadership and organization to keep everything in place yet moving forward.

Today's parish is culturally and generationally diverse. Most parishes in the United States are presently serving six generations. Add to this complexity the many immigrants who are part of parish communities bringing diverse gifts, as well as the challenges of language and spiritual and temporal needs. All of this adds to the urgency of being intentional about ministry.

A People

Someone once said that the three most important words that describe parish are "relationships, relationships, relationships"! Our understanding of parish comes from the call of the community, as in ancient Israel. This is an assembly of people, a chosen people, called together by God, to be in communion with God and each other in Christ to continue the mission. When leaders understand relationship-building, it is a most powerful force. Parishes need to develop ways to be welcoming, hospitable, engaging, and inclusive to meet the needs of everyone. If there are new immigrants in sizable numbers moving in, it will be important to have the Eucharistic liturgy in their language — and not relegated to an obscure time slot or a building with no air conditioning. Hospitality is the ability and the creativity to welcome all, even the most marginalized, into our community.

What do the people most appreciate besides a welcoming and supportive spirit? It is a prayerful Eucharistic liturgy with good music and the great preaching. This is where Christ is made real in the Word, Sacrament, and the assembly. It is the joy of the community, the place where they gather to meet the Lord and each other at the deepest level of communion — the place where all are welcome.

Mission

In my travels around the country, I find that parishes are not always clear about their mission. Parishes are busy, of course, but perhaps without enough of a focus or a vision about what they are doing. Pastors and staff often say that they are so overwhelmed by all the people they need to minister to and all the things that need to be done that they have no time to focus. As one person said, "We're way too busy to be planning around here!"

This attitude, understandable as it may be, is not helpful for parish success. Pastors and parish leaders must take time to step back and reflect on the mission of their parish. Each parish is unique and serves a unique group of people. What works in one parish may work differently in the neighboring parish. Leaders can discover the focus of mission by gathering folks to talk and reflect. Due to our increasingly secular culture and the times we live in, ongoing theological reflection is needed to make the Gospel heard. This can be done on several levels: *Scriptural Reflection:* What is the mission of Jesus? *Theological Reflection:* What is the mission of Jesus at this particular time and in today's culture? As a parish, what is our reason for being? How does Jesus call us to participate in the mission? *Practical Reflection:* What is our mission in this parish? How will we advance the mission of Jesus? What is our vision? The successful parish takes time to do these kinds of reflection and uses processes that include as many people as possible.

A Structure

The successful parish sees itself as a place to develop leadership. The pastor or parish life coordinator is the appointed leader and needs to understand what leadership is, how to be a leader, and how to share leadership with others. Leadership does not mean that one person does everything. Rather, the leader sets the direction, creates visions and goals collaboratively, and then keeps them going. The unsuccessful parish puts out fires without asking how they were started. On the other hand, the successful parish has plans for emergencies as well as an overall vision.

The role of the parish pastoral council is to keep developing the vision through ongoing assessments and evaluations of the ministry. The council is the key structure to encourage participation and training by setting goals and policies that ensure that the parishioners are equipped spiritually so that they, too, can carry out the mission of Christ in their families, neighborhood, workplace, and everyday social encounters.

Finally, a parish evaluates its effectiveness in all areas: the pastor, parish life coordinator, staff, ministers, ministries, and programs. Several dioceses have developed self-evaluation tools for pastors and other ministers, as well as overall parish evaluations. But they are not used enough! Evaluation is a key instrument for assessing the effectiveness of the ministry and for setting the parish's vision and direction.

All of these characteristics are essential to the life of a parish. Today parishes are merging, clustering, partnering, building new churches, sharing a priest, without a resident priest, with a parish life coordinator, with a homogeneous community or with a multicultural community. There are so many different styles, but what matters is that all parishes are doing the work of Jesus Christ and should be intentional about doing excellent ministry.

Covenant

In this book Tom Sweetser challenges the intentional or "successful" parish to go to a higher level. By understanding the notion
of covenant, we begin to understand the sacred trust that is the
parish. Sharing authority, being collaborative, creating community,
and building vital and significant ministries is what the church
needs. If we do not develop this sense of covenant in our parishes
for all generations, we may find ourselves a remnant people rather
than alive, purposeful disciples of Jesus Christ. We need to *choose.*

In closing, I must say that I am honored to be asked by Tom
Sweetser to add my thoughts to this wonderful book. Through his
writings, workshops, and years of contact with me, he has served
as a mentor to me on parish life and development, urging me to
have a keen pastoral eye to what works well and what needs to be
encouraged. Thinking about the message of *Keeping the Covenant,* I
would also like to mention two other great mentors in my life. One
is Monsignor Thomas Kleissler, with whom I worked in a parish in
Newark and later with RENEW in both U.S. dioceses and abroad.
Tom taught me leadership skills and showed me that so much was
possible with solid leadership and engaged parishioners. The second
is Monsignor Philip Murnion, who mentored me for over a decade
before I came to the National Pastoral Life Center. For another
decade until his untimely death, we worked closely with parishes
and dioceses to raise the essential questions around parish ministry
and to urge them to do their best for the sake of the mission of
Jesus. For me, these men form a trinity of dedication to the mission.

Donna L. Ciangio, O.P.
Church Leadership Consultation
West Caldwell, New Jersey

Introduction

The king directed that all the elders of Judah and Jerusalem should be gathered to him. The king went up to the house of the Lord, and with him went all the people of Judah, all the inhabitants of Jerusalem, the priests, the prophets, and all the people, both small and great; he read in their hearing all the words of the book of the covenant that had been found in the house of the Lord. The king stood by the pillar and made a covenant before the Lord, to follow the Lord, keeping his commandments, his decrees, and his statues, with all his heart and all his soul, to perform the words of this covenant that were written in this book. All the people joined in the covenant.   — 2 Kings 23:1–3

A covenant is more than a contract. It is a commitment of the heart, a pledge to be faithful to the other. Yahweh renews again and again the covenant, the commitment, with the Chosen. "I will make a covenant of peace with them; it shall be an everlasting covenant with them; and I will bless them and multiply them and will set my sanctuary among them forevermore. My dwelling place shall be with them; and I will be their God, and they shall be my people" (Ezek. 37:26–27).

This covenant between God and people, this love relationship, was carried to new depths in the life, death, and resurrection of Jesus, God's son. No longer was it just the Hebrews who were

1

the Chosen. All who accepted Jesus as their God and Savior were drawn into this love relationship.

Baptism is the ritual sign of this covenant. The church is the framework out of which this sign takes shape, and parish is the place where it happens. Each individual experiences the waters of baptism, but it is done in the midst of an assembly, a Chosen People. The parish itself is a covenant, not just an organization or a structure. It is the place where the personal invitation of God to share a new way of living is linked to a people willing to give themselves over to this commitment of faith and loving service. The parish is the place where people come together each week to discover more and more about who this God is in their lives. They are nourished by Word and Sacrament. They praise God and acknowledge Jesus as their friend and savior. They do this as a "we" and not as a collection of individuals.

The covenantal relationship between God and the parish community flows deep. "I will be their God and they shall be my people." There are moments where this becomes manifest. The pastor preaches an inspiring homily asking forgiveness for abuses in the church and the congregation gives him a standing ovation, bringing tears to his eyes. A beloved staff member dies unexpectedly and the parishioners pour out feelings of love and appreciation at the wake and funeral. A children's choir sings at Christmas Eve Mass with such clarity and simplicity that the church falls silent before the mystery of the Incarnation. A deacon holds up his own grandchild for all in the assembly to see, having just baptized the child through immersion. Two teenagers give a witness talk during Mass after returning from a work camp in Mexico. Their conversion experience so affects the congregation that the second collection for the Mexican parish brings in thousands of dollars. The painful closing of a mission church is easier to bear because of the open-hearted welcome by those at the new place of worship. The covenant runs deep. God is made present through the undying faith and loving service of the People of God.

Expanding the Covenant

The covenant is more than the mutual commitment of God and People. This relationship is repeated on many levels and between many groups and individuals. The pastor, for instance, models the covenant by entering into a partnership with one other person so that together they give direction and leadership to the parish. This partnership, or "dual focus," around which the parish revolves is now not just one person but two individuals. Both pastor and the other person form a dual leadership role, each one with a defined set of duties and responsibilities, as well as a particular sphere of activity and influence. Who this other person might be depends on each parish situation. It could be a parish administrator, a pastoral associate, a parochial vicar, or a deacon. Whoever it might be, the pastor is willing to share his own authority for running the parish with another, thus entering into a mutual relationship of accountability, that is, into a covenant with this other person.

Because the pastor is canonically "the head of the parish," he has the ability to share this role with another person, someone who takes the burden of administration, personnel, and finances off his shoulders. The pastors who have entered into partnership with one, or in some cases, two other persons, have found it a freeing and exhilarating experience. This mutual relationship also encourages others to work in partnership as well. Examples include various staff members working on projects together, parish groups and ministries being led by co-chairs and not by a single individual, staff members empowering parishioners to plan and direct projects and programs *with* them rather than being the only person in charge. All of these efforts at sharing power and authority are manifestations of the covenantal relationship between God and People. The parish makes visible, in a myriad of ways that "we are in this together." By being in partnership with others we enter into God's life and God chooses to share life with us.

3

Faced with Reality

This is the ideal. The reality often falls short of this. At the present time so much pulls the parish down and makes it face its own failings, limitations, and inadequacies. The humanness of the church is all too obvious. Priests have been removed from ministry because of inappropriate behavior. Parish groups and individuals are at odds with one another over the smallest of issues. Staff members are in conflict; pastoral council members and other parish leaders become disillusioned and frustrated. Parishioners pull back from participation and involvement. Leaders in the church abuse their power and authority, causing scandal and hardship to the faithful. The covenant between God and People, and among the people themselves, is strained to the breaking point.

Some of the best trained and most capable parish staff members, as well as loyal lay leaders, are withdrawing. They are rethinking their involvement and commitment to a church that uses their talents and energies but offers little in return. This is especially true for women. They make up the vast majority of the workforce in the church, but they are given little or no voice in how it is being run. One gifted pastoral associate, who was the glue that kept the staff and parish together, confided that she had trouble attending Mass because it meant participating in a church ritual that professed one thing — love and equality — while the institutional church practiced just the opposite.

Over the last few years, longtime and faithful parishioners have been dropping out. Instead of attending Mass every week, as they had done for years, they now attend once or twice a month, if that. They are losing interest as their faith in the church wanes. They will attend a special liturgy that speaks to their interests or search for a parish and presider that touch their spiritual hunger, but they are no longer regular attendees. And with their withdrawal comes a drop in parish finances. For the first time since the Gallup Organization has been keeping records, the level of Catholic church attendance has fallen below the Protestant average. And there is no upward trend in sight. Yes, the American Catholic Church is in serious trouble. But with every crisis comes opportunity. The mystery is that new life continues to come forth from the pain and struggle. God never lets go, never. People do, but not God. The offer of divine life remains. It is up to the parish, especially its leadership, to hang on and keep the promise of the covenant alive. This book offers suggestions on how this can be accomplished. It is based on direct experience over many years with parishes across the country, always looking for what works and what could be improved. There is not, of course, one way of being parish, but the core of each and every one is the same reality, God desiring to enter into a loving relationship with us and a free choice on our part to respond to this invitation. The parish provides a place for this to happen — a locus, a haven, a framework, a prod, a help, a model, a host where people learn, grow, celebrate, and share God's life within and among themselves and with others.

How This Book Is Structured

This book contains five sections, each one emphasizing an aspect of parish that can take it to the next level. Within each section are four or five chapters that are short enough so they can be used for group discussion, either by staff, council, commissions, parishioners, or participants in classes and seminars. At the end of each chapter are two questions to help focus the discussion. An individual reader might also find the questions helpful in shaping personal reflection or for uncovering next steps for further action in one's own life or in the parish.

This is, in other words, a "hands-on" book, meant to provide avenues for parish renewal and conversion. It offers suggestions and ideas for making the parish a viable institution for communal worship, relation-building, faith enrichment, Christian service, and servant leadership. Underneath all this activity and ministry is the same central focus, a giving of oneself to God and to others in a covenantal relationship. Only then can the parish move to the next level in its growth cycle, a step the Spirit of God keeps calling and inviting it to take.

Section One

Experiencing Covenant: What Drives Us

Nothing is more practical than finding God, that is, than falling in love in a quite absolute, final way. What you are in love with, what seizes your imagination, will affect everything. It will decide

> what will get you out of bed in the morning,
>
> what you do with your evenings,
>
> how you spend your weekends,
>
> what you read, who you know,
>
> what breaks your heart,
>
> and what amazes you with joy and gratitude.

Fall in love, stay in love, and it will decide everything.

— Attributed to Pedro Arrupe, S.J.,
former Superior General of the Society of Jesus

Chapter One

Making a Difference

One person can make a difference in a parish, and it does not have to be the pastor. Someone with a vision, a hope, a desire, and a commitment can change everything. One individual is willing to say, "I am not giving up on this parish, this council, this staff, this pastor. There is much that needs changing, but there is good here as well. God has not given up on this place; neither will I." The commitment starts with prayer, every day — same place, same time — a chance to be still and know that God is near. This is where the covenant is found: showing up each day, pouring out one's longings and desires, and then letting God do the rest.

The next step is to be attentive to what is going on around you, especially in the life of the parish. Allow the little nudges, intuitions, and inspirations to guide you. An assistant music director knows that so much more could be done to bring life to the weekend liturgies but has no idea how to begin. She has no power and little influence. In desperation she enrolls in a class at the local seminary and is filled with new and promising ideas and suggestions. When she brings it back to the staff it falls on deaf ears. Undaunted she tries out new music at the one weekend Mass she directs, songs that can be sung in rounds, alternating verses between one side and the other or between men and women, even a simple song done in parts for the entire congregation to try out.

The assembly begins to catch on and the choir becomes encouraged. The presider picks up on the new spirit of the people, and as a result the Mass begins to have new life and energy to it. The one in charge of music takes note and starts to incorporate this new approach to congregational involvement in the other liturgies as well. A sense of hope and future begins to take hold in the staff. The assistant music director is amazed at what is happening as a result of her small attempts to bring life to one of the Masses.

A parish secretary knows the staff is not working well together. She can sense the tension underneath the pleasantries staff members exchange in their interactions with one another. She has no idea how to confront the issue; she isn't even invited to staff meetings. She knows the needs of parishioners are not being served when phone calls are not returned or when she is unable to locate staff members when people come looking for information and assistance.

At a loss about what to do, she contacts the former pastor, who is retired and living in another parish. He invites her to come over for what he describes as a "strategy session." The two of them sit down with a Bible and spend time praying over what options she might have to ease the conflicts and tension on staff.

"It's not just the staff," the secretary complains. "It's the whole parish that is being affected."

Her confidant surprised her by asking, "What's right with the staff? Let's support and celebrate that."

After some prodding, she began listing some attributes such as hardworking, dedicated, committed, skilled, well-informed, and self-directed. As the former pastor asked for more that was going right with the staff, the secretary could see that the real issue was no accountability to one another. Each person on staff was working independently of the others, totally absorbed in what he or she was doing. The staff meetings were only reports of each other's activities without any time for bonding, giving feedback, or coming to a consensus on important matters. The current pastor, being an

10

introvert and somewhat shy, was either unable or unwilling to challenge staff members to work more as a group and not independently of one another. What to do?

After some soul-searching and brainstorming by the two of them, the secretary came up with a suggestion. "I can't do much with the staff," she said. "I am not in a position to influence their meetings or interaction. But I can provide a model of how to work better together. There are five of us in support positions who could get together and form our own little group. These include Charlie, the maintenance person, Joyce and Irene, the religious education secretaries, Joan, the bookkeeper, and myself. If the pastor gives his approval, I could call them together and share ideas about how to make the administration run more smoothly. I should probably include someone from the regular staff to make it look official, perhaps Jerry, the permanent deacon. He has complained to me about how splintered the staff is. He told me that he takes a back seat at staff meetings because he is so discouraged by the lack of unity and cohesion. He could keep the staff informed about what we are doing."

The secretary returned to her job with new hope and determination. With the pastor's blessing, she took the initiative to call the other five together for a meeting. To her surprise and delight, all of them caught on to her idea and made a commitment to meet every other week to share ideas about how to make their work and ministry more productive and responsive to others. They wanted to do more than just report on what they were doing. They saw this as a chance to get to know each other, look at how they were functioning as support staff and make changes for the better. It wasn't long before the pastoral staff took notice and wanted to know what the support staff was doing at their meetings. Whatever it was, it became obvious that more and better work was coming out of their deliberations.

Consider a member of the pastoral council. Harry had been a member for five years because no one could be found to take his place. He could see why. The monthly meetings were long, boring, and unproductive. The pastor had made it clear that the council was "advisory only," which made the meetings difficult to endure and attendance a problem. On most occasions there were no agenda items prepared ahead of time. The chairperson opened the meeting, the pastor led the prayer, and then he brought up issues that were on his mind, asking the group to give him counsel and advice. The pastor listened well to everyone's wisdom, thanked them for their input, and then went on to the next issue. Quite often there would be reports made by various parish groups and organizations or people presenting requests for new projects and programs. What was frustrating is that those making the presentations thought the council was the decider about whether to go ahead or not. That is what it looked like on the surface, but in reality the membership watched for the pastor's reaction and, reading his body language, voted accordingly.

To Harry, it was a colossal waste of time and energy. He had stuck it out this long because he liked the pastor and knew that the feeling was mutual. But it was becoming more than he could bear. In desperation, he began reading books and articles related to parishes and about pastoral councils in particular. As he did so, he discovered options for running meetings and ways to make the council a more collaborative effort of pastor and members working in partnership. As he gained this new knowledge he wondered how to approach the pastor about his insights and discoveries. He decided to take a risk and invite him out for lunch at a nice restaurant, just the two of them, as a way of broaching the topic.

The pastor took him up on the offer, saying that he wanted to talk over some issues related to the council. Harry was delighted at the response he received from the pastor, but what happened over lunch was a complete surprise. What the pastor wanted to talk about was a change in how the council functioned.

"The meetings," the pastor began, "are going nowhere. Nothing is getting accomplished and I find them a waste of my time, and yours as well. What can we do to make them more productive and enjoyable?"

That was the opening Harry needed. "As long as you asked, Father, I think we need a complete change of perspective. If you will excuse the expression, all of us are merely 'yes people' to your wishes. We don't feel free to speak our minds. We all wait to see what you want. It is not doing its job, at least as I've been able to discover from some of the reading I've been doing." Harry said all this with some trepidation, but he felt that if he didn't say it now he never would. To his great surprise the pastor asked, "What are you reading, Harry? Can you show me what you have?"

What followed that lunch was a complete change of mind-set by the pastor. Council members were amazed at the shift they experienced at the next meeting. The pastor explained that he would no longer be merely asking advice but would like everyone to be an equal member with him in coming to a consensus on issues. "I'm not the only one who can make decisions," he confessed. "We can do this together. We also need a new way of operating. I've asked Harry to work with Andy as partners. The two of them will co-chair the meetings together and will work with me to set up a good agenda for the meetings. You will all get the agenda beforehand via email. We have a ways to go, but this change will help us get started. Are you with me?"

No one responded immediately; they were too stunned to reply. But change they did, and the council meetings have set a new tone and direction for all the other groups in the parish as well. Harry still shakes his head in wonderment at what a little risk-taking will produce.

Consider these three people who made a difference — an assistant music director, a parish secretary, and a pastoral council member. Each one sensed a problem and decided to do something about it. They were faith-filled people who prayed about what to do and responded to the promptings within them. There was a covenant of risk-taking and initiative going on inside, a hidden conversation with the Spirit of hope and promise deep within.

Next came action. For the assistant music director it was trying out new ways to do the music. She and the congregation entered into a covenant of communal worship through uplifting and inviting music. Together, with her encouragement and direction, the people were making new music before the Lord.

For the secretary, the covenant was first with the retired pastor, who provided the support and encouragement she needed to try out something beyond what she thought she could do. The second covenantal relationship was with the support staff as they came together for mutual planning and creative problem solving.

As for Harry, he was aware something was not working. This led him to seek out resources and new insights. He discovered books and resources that gave him new information. Then came the eventful meal with the pastor. Both he and the pastor were ready for change, but it was his initiative and new knowledge that got the ball rolling. This is the first step in taking the parish to the next level. Someone, anyone, needs to believe it can happen and be willing to take the first step in that direction. In the words of DeWitt Jones from the video *Celebrate What Is Right in the World,* "If you believe it, you will see it."[1]

Questions

1. What is God asking of you in your parish?

2. "If you believe it, you will see it." What do you believe the parish can become?

Chapter Two

Why a Parish?

Why have parishes at all? Why not enter into a covenant with God on your own and leave it at that? The parish is such a hassle; so much work and so little to show for it. Is it really necessary? After all, the majority of the parishioners don't show up for church anymore, except on Easter and Christmas, or for weddings and funerals. Would anyone miss it if it stopped operating? There is, of course, always an outcry if a parish is threatened with closure, but isn't the protest mostly for nostalgic reasons? "It's where I was baptized and got married; I want to be buried from there as well!" So why have a parish? What does it do? Why is it important?

Each one of us enters into a personal relationship with God deep within the recesses of our being. It is a personal, intimate, mysterious experience that includes invitation and response, ecstasy and struggle, darkness and light, awareness and unknowing. There is a freeing, creative, dynamic force to this encounter that is personal and unique to each individual. The parish is the place where the expression of our deepest longings is made manifest in communal prayer and worship, in faith enrichment and development, in outreach to the poor and needy, in the call to just and moral behavior — all done with others in a structured, communal setting. We all need help, in various ways and stages of life, to discover God in our lives and to develop our unique relationship with the divine life within.

15

Coping with the messiness of our lives and trying to overcome our self-seeking tendencies require great conviction, determination, and discipline, something most of us don't have, at least not for very long. We need help; we need parish. Also, throughout our lives, key moments of personal covenant need a community with which to share the joys and sorrows of the moment, a people of faith who rejoice with us at our loves and triumphs, grieve with us at our losses and failures. For this, too, we need parish. When we experience injustice, are indignant when human rights are ignored, or feel helpless in the face of immoral and self-seeking institutions, the parish is a place to join forces against oppression, to bear witness to God's action in the world, to stand up for what is right and just, not alone but in solidarity with those who share the same faith and commitment. The parish, in other words, is not a bureaucratic, controlling religious organization of rules and regulations. It is a living, breathing body of people who invite, support, challenge, and forgive one another through word, code, and ritual. The covenant within each person meets the larger covenant residing in the parish community. The two reinforce, strengthen, and make visible a mystery that is difficult to define or explain but is real and tangible to those who share a bond of faith and commitment. This, in its best and worst moments, is parish.

A Few Examples

Consider the woman who wakes up on Sunday morning and says to herself, "I don't want to go to church. The music is a performance, the priest is predictable, the community is cold, and the environment is sterile. I'll just spend time in personal prayer instead." For some unknown reason — call it the urging of an inner covenant — by the end of the day she decides to go anyway. She strikes out for the Sunday evening Mass, one she had not attended before. To her amazement, her predictions did not come true. As she approached the church building, greeters — mostly young people — were at the doors welcoming people into the assembly, smiling, shaking hands, and offering song books to each person who entered. "I've never had this happen to me before," she reflects. "Where did all this come from?"

Music was playing as she entered, soothing, meditative music that gave her a sense of awe and reverence. That, too, was new to her. As the congregation stood to welcome the celebrant, a song leader encouraged all to sing, supported by members of the choir who stood along the aisles so that the voice of the people was much fuller and more alive than she had experienced in the past. She knew the hymn and broke into song with enthusiasm, catching the spirit of the choir members standing close by.

The celebrant had a friendly manner that seemed inviting and inclusive. His simple greeting and smile spoke volumes to her. "He's much better than I remember him being at the Mass I usually attend," she mused. The rest of the service was a pure gift to her, from the way the readings were proclaimed to the engaging homily, from the shared petitions where she could speak her need for prayers with the person next to her, to the greeting of peace that was more than just a perfunctory handshake or nod.

On returning home, she felt she had experienced God in a new way. The liturgy had given her strength to face the coming week with renewed determination and commitment. She found herself saying, "Why have I not gone to this Mass before? What led me there today? This was just what I needed. I certainly want to try that out again."

In another parish the director of religious formation was frustrated because the parents dropped off their children on Sunday morning for religious education classes and then disappeared. Only a few showed up for the adult discussion session that took place at the same time. She wasn't even sure those dropping off their children even attended Mass. One Sunday morning, as she went out to her car to get some books she had forgotten, she noticed people sitting in their cars reading the Sunday newspaper or doing other tasks. She became curious and decided to count how many there were — twenty-three cars in all. Something was wrong with this picture. Obviously the adult enrichment session inside was not in tune with the interests and desires of those out in the parking lot. Reading the paper was more rewarding that talking about an aspect of faith, parenting, or some world issue. The next Sunday, as soon as the classes were in session and she had an extra moment, she got a large tray, piled it high with donuts, added a coffee pot, and some paper cups, and headed for the parking lot. She went from car to car, offering free coffee and a donut — no questions asked. "That was fun," she concluded as she returned to her office. "I had always wanted to be a carhop."

What she discovered as she made her rounds, and people got over their initial surprise, was that they were willing to talk with her as she provided the refreshments. It broke the ice, and the parents started to ask questions about their children. "How's he doing? He never says much when I pick him up." "I have to tell you, Sally is not getting much out of her classes. Says it's 'bo-ring' as any child her age would do. Is there anything I can do to get her more interested?" "My son likes his teacher but so few show up for the class. He feels as if he's the only one who's faithful. What can you do to encourage the children to show up each week?" These questions showed her that what would bring people out of their cars and into the adult sharing session would be less emphasis on theology and more on issues facing parents as they try to raise children in a challenging environment.

So this is what she did — not that everyone picked up on her offer. Some still kept to themselves and stayed in their cars. She got a few teens to make the rounds in the parking lot, providing coffee and donuts and even selling the Sunday newspaper to those who stayed put. But for those who did take her up on the chance to talk about their children and their faith development, the experience turned out to be far more enjoyable than an hour sitting in their cars each Sunday morning. A new aspect of parish was taking shape.

Why Parish?

The two examples, and many others like them, answer the question, "Why parish?" It meets a need and offers an outlet for a God-experience and mutual bonding with others that is more than an individual or a family can do on its own. As Moses said to the Israelites, "You are a people, holy to the Lord your God, the Lord your God has chosen you out of all the peoples on earth to be his people, his treasured possession" (Deut. 7:6). Parish is a *People* seeking to respond to the invitation of encounter and relationship. When we least expect it, parish becomes grace, makes sense, is what we long for and desire. For those moments, we are forever grateful.

Questions

1. Name a moment in your life when parish made sense to you and made all the difference.

2. Describe the parish of your dreams and how it provides a framework for people's experience of God in their lives.

Chapter Three

On a Mission

A parish does not exist of and for itself. It is not a place where people come to have merely their own needs met, at least not a parish that is alive and active. It is on a mission. Everyone who comes in contact with the parish is forever changed, transformed from a consumer to a giver. Nice theory, but can it really happen? "If you believe it," DeWitt Jones says, "you will see it."[2] John F. Kennedy challenged the country in 1961, "Ask what you can do for your county." This is what Jesus called his followers to do in John's Gospel, "If I wash your feet, you must wash one another's feet" (John 13).

A choir director became discouraged with the conduct of some of the choir members during Mass. It was a great group of singers. The practices were delightful experiences of people learning new harmonies and having fun singing with one another. The only difficulty was that this same attitude carried over to the weekend Masses as well. Choir members were not disrespectful so much as not paying attention to what was going on in the liturgy. They spent most of the time searching for music to get ready for the next song or making side comments to one another, especially during the homily. Receiving Communion seemed to be a perfunctory gesture that came between the Lamb of God and the Communion song. The choir members came more for their own enjoyment than from a desire to lead the congregation in song. The director brought up his concern at the next staff meeting. "What can I do to get across to the choir that this is not a performance but a ministry? How can I give them a new sense of purpose, an awareness that they are part of a deeper mystery called Eucharist?"

"What about us?" the principal spoke up. "Do we have a good sense of our own purpose as a staff, or are we just running from one thing to another, overwhelmed by all that has to get done? I have the same sense about the teachers. Most of them do a great job in the classroom, but when we get together for faculty meetings, it seems no different than the public school I was in before coming here. It should make a difference that we are a parish school."

The pastor listened intently to this discussion, knowing it was striking a chord within him as well. Something was gnawing at him about the pastoral council meeting the night before. It was an efficient and productive meeting with good ideas around the table on every topic. But there was no sense of *why* it had come together as a council, no struggle about who they were as leaders in the parish, nobody asking the deeper questions about purpose or overall direction. He couldn't help wonder whether he was at fault for not challenging the council more. But he was worn out after a long day, and he didn't have the energy to raise the issue. Now, however, as the choir director and principal were talking he started to get interested in trying out something different.

"You know what?" he began. "We haven't been away for a staff day in a long time. Let's set one up so we can really tackle this issue of purpose and motivation. It would be good for us as well, and for the people we serve in our ministries."

All agreed, and after some difficult negotiating to find a time all were free, the staff gathered for its day away. Two people agreed to plan the agenda and guide the discussion. They came up with the theme: "It's all about mission: we're here for others, not ourselves." Staff members were asked to pray ahead of time on this theme and to bring along a scripture quote, an article, or a chapter from a book that would shed light on the subject. The day began with group prayer and petitions for a successful day. Staff members then split up into pairs to share their insights about being on mission, as well as sharing with each other the resources they had brought with them. After half an hour, the entire staff regrouped to share the results of their one-on-one reflection. The discussion went for two solid hours. Staff members were so absorbed by the interchange that they pushed lunch back thirty minutes because no one wanted to break the momentum.

What was so captivating was a possible shift in emphasis and way of operating. "We all need to buy into the same mission, the same reason for doing what we are doing," the youth minister blurted out. "What will get us through the tough days? What will stir us into action? What will focus our prayer and deliberations together? Let's name it!"

The staff caught the enthusiasm of the youth minister as everyone tried to articulate their reason for being on staff. Was it to lead a ministry? No, it came out of something deeper. Was it to spread the Good News as Jesus had instructed? Yes, perhaps, but this didn't grab the group's imagination; it was too vague to motivate them. Was it to model Christ's love among themselves and with others? Yes, that was a start, but something was missing. To be disciples? To be sent? To call others to ministry and service? To be a person for others?

The staff could sense they were getting closer, but their mission and purpose still eluded them. Then the secretary mentioned, almost sheepishly, "Aren't we here to set people free so they can be on a mission as well? Isn't our purpose as staff members to not get in the way of people's call, to provide the occasion and opportunity for people to be followers of Christ in active, concrete ways? We are here to invite, challenge, and coach, not to do it *for* them but rather to do it *with* them. Isn't that why I answer the phone the way I do and direct people to someone from whom they can get answers or needed assistance? But is this the best way to handle their concerns and issues? We are here to give people freedom, not make them dependent upon us or make them jump through a lot of hoops."

Everyone turned to the secretary and yelled, "That's it! Good for you. Our mission is to free people to follow Christ by being *for others,* just as we ourselves seek to do the same. We are here to keep the 'Giving Cycle' going, keep passing it on."

Lunch was a lively affair; people were happy with their new insight and discovery. The secretary was given the place of honor at the table for breaking the logjam and shaping their mission and purpose. The afternoon was spent on planning ways to implement their new understanding of themselves.

"First," the pastor began, "comes the pastoral council. I feel somewhat uneasy that we not lay this new 'mission' on the council members without their involvement and consultation."

"No problem," the religious education director replied. "If we are about freeing people to answer the call, then we need to invite the council to go through the very same process of discovery as we have done. We had a good agenda for today's gathering. Could you do the same with the council on a Saturday morning or Sunday afternoon?" "Yes, I think I could do that," the pastor responded, "only I don't want to lead it. I'm not good at that. Would the two who planned this day do the same for the council?"

"Yes, indeed; we would be delighted," the planners volunteered. "Poll the council membership and see when this could happen. We will take it from there. If our mission is to 'free people so they can answer the call to be there for others,' we can start with the council as well as with anyone else."

"And I can start with the choir as well," the music director piped up. "What would free them so they can be a choir *for others* and not just so they can have a good time among themselves? I think I'll start the way we did here. At the next practice I will tell them about our staff day and then invite them to reflect over the next week why we have a choir, what is its purpose and function. I might even give them a short article to read. The next week I'm going to call off practicing music and spend the time on group discussion instead. I know some may not like it, but we have to start somewhere. I will begin the session with prayer, perhaps joining hands around the altar and ending the prayer with a song they all like to sing. After that I'll send them off in pairs to reflect on the purpose of the choir, especially how they could be there for others in this special ministry. Then I will call them back together to see what was discussed. My hope is that they will redirect their efforts to connect with the congregation more, getting the assembly to sing rather than listen to our lovely voices. Maybe we could incorporate some quiet time, both during the practices and at Mass, so that choir members have a chance to pray quietly as well as 'make joyful noise' together. This is going to be risky business. Wish me luck."

The principal chimed in and committed herself to "be a 'freer' of the faculty," as she put it. "We have to go away as a group just as we have done today. Our teacher in-service sessions have never dealt with the spiritual side of our work. It will now. At our next faculty meeting I'm going to share with them what happened here and invite them to reflect on what makes this school different from every other school. Are we really freeing our children — parents, too — to use their gifts *for others*, or just to get ahead? Competition is strong in the upper grades. I'm going to ask the faculty how we could turn this on its head and encourage students to allow others to get ahead, or even help others win and succeed. What a shift that would be! The faculty itself must look at competition among its own members and model partnership instead of one-upmanship. This is a tough lesson to learn, but this process might just do it. I'll let you know what happens."

At this, the pastoral associate spoke up, somewhat hesitantly. "I'm in charge of all the liturgical ministers except music. How can I get across to the ushers, for instance, that they are not 'in charge' of seating but are called to be there *for others*? What will free up that group I wonder. But you know, getting them together and having them reflect on their purpose and mission might just do it. Perhaps I could call all the liturgical ministers together for a 'Mission Meeting.' Split them up into ushers, lectors, Eucharistic ministers, greeters — the works. I could meet ahead of time with the heads of each ministry and train them in this process. When we have the gathering, we could start with sending people off in pairs to reflect on what is the ministry of their particular group, such as the mission of lectoring or serving or taking up the collection. We could get them into ministry groupings to see what the pairs come up with. It might surprise us all, ushers included. It's worth a try. Anybody here willing to help me out with this?"

"We could all help out," the youth minister suggested. "Each one of us could be a partner with the head of a liturgical ministry and help them with the group discussion. We might learn a thing or two ourselves. To experience all the ministers at a given Mass "on a mission" will be quite a sight to behold. Our weekend liturgies will never be the same."

"Wonderful," the pastoral associate exclaimed. "What a difference this will make, not just to the liturgical ministers but to the congregation as a whole. Imagine what it will look like if people catch on to this new way of worshiping as help for living their lives *for others* instead of fulfilling an obligation.

Reflecting on the Experience

A few essential ingredients made this staff conversion possible. First came a willingness to "risk the unfamiliar." The music director took a risk in bringing up a concern at the staff meeting. The principal risked telling the staff her misgivings about the faculty. The pastor admitted feeling the need for something different at the council meetings. The status quo wasn't working, at least not to these three persons' satisfaction.

Next came a process, a framework for "how to proceed." A few planners put together the staff day, which included prayer, personal reflection, one-on-one sharing, and finally large group discussion.

The process helped create a safe environment in which all felt free to share their thoughts and feelings. Greater trust was the fruit of good planning. The planners also created a theme for the day: "It's all about mission; we are here for others, not ourselves." This helped focus the discussion. The group itself, however, was flexible enough to stay with the theme until they hit upon a solution, the insight provided by the secretary. That was the "tipping point." The rest was easy, putting the agreed-upon "mission" into action in each person's ministry. The ramifications of this "day away" spread throughout the parish. It become a model to the council, choir, school faculty, and liturgical ministers. Once they caught the spirit, it spread to other ministers and parishioners as well.

In summary, the steps included:

1. Experiencing a need or frustration

2. Taking the risk of mentioning this to others

3. Designing a process to discover a solution

4. Creating a focus for personal reflection, group discussion, and sharing ideas

5. Staying with it until a solution is discovered, one that all can own and buy in to

6. Putting the solution into action by designing steps for implementation

Questions

1. What concrete steps would need to be taken to move your group or ministry into a sense of "being on a mission"?

2. How could being more aware and clear about your mission and purpose change the way you do your work or ministry?

Chapter Four

Creating a Mission Statement

How does a parish go about defining its purpose and mission, how does it discover and articulate its core values and essential ingredients? One place to begin is with the pastoral council, which includes the pastor as an integral member. Consider a council meeting at which one of the members brings up a question someone asked her after Mass.

"Jan, you're on the council. Do you ever discuss what is special about our parish, what makes us different from all the other parishes in town? I know each one is unique, but I was just wondering if it's written down anywhere just what is different about us. I read the mission statement on the cover of the bulletin, but that doesn't tell me much. Where else can I look?"

Jan was not able to find anything in her notes from past meetings that would satisfy the woman's inquiry, so she brought it up at the next council meeting. "What do I tell her? Where should I look? I'm at a loss here."

The rest of the council did the typical reaction; they all turned to the pastor for the answer. He laughed at their consternation, then gave a shrug, and said, "You know, I'm not sure we do have a list of what makes our parish unique and special. The mission statement has been around for a while, but your questioner is right. I don't know where to turn to help her out. Maybe we should look into this for our next meeting."

Secretly he was delighted the subject had come up. This, in his mind, was just what a council was for, to articulate the core values of the parish. As he looked around the room, he could see interest on the faces of the council members. But he also sensed a hesitation and reluctance to delve into such a massive project at the next meeting — discovering the core values of the parish. Where to start, how to proceed?

As a way of quelling his own and others' anxiety, the pastor suggested, "What an excellent opportunity for us. It could be a real moment of grace, both for us and the parish. Can I suggest that a few of you meet with me to work out how we could go about this? It might even take an extra meeting of the council so we can give this the time and attention it deserves. Perhaps we could put aside a few hours on a Saturday morning. I would also like to call the staff in on this. You and the staff working together should be able to arrive at something really good. We haven't had a joint meeting with them for some time. Are there any volunteers who could help me out with this?"

The pastor was surprised at how many hands shot up, almost half of the council. He picked Jan, who initiated the conversation, and Jonathan, a sociology teacher who had a good sense of group process. Not to let the moment pass, the pastor took out his scheduler and suggested the Saturday after Labor Day as a possible date for the council/staff gathering. Not everyone was able to make a commitment on the spot, but the energy level was soaring. People were enthusiastic about what happened at this meeting and wanted to follow up on the conversation as soon as possible.

The subcommittee of three agreed to meet within the week, and the pastor suggested adding a staff member to the meeting as a way of getting the staff on board. This turn of events was completely unexpected, but as he left the council meeting his spirits were high. "I've not seen such spark at a council meeting for a long time," he thought to himself. "This could lead to something very good for us as a council, and for the parish as well."

28

At the next staff meeting the pastor reported what had happened at the council meeting. "I hope you don't mind, but I committed you to a joint meeting with the council to work out some of our core values as a parish. We have been talking about this among ourselves for some time, but nothing has developed. Now is our chance. What about it? Are you game?"

"Sounds like fun," Jerry, the young adult minister responded. "I would like to do this with our own planning team as well. It's always good to get under the surface and talk about *why* we are doing what we are doing." Others on staff were also open to this invitation to be part of the council's project. It was Jerry who agreed to join the committee that was working out the agenda for the special session.

As the pastor, the two council members, and staff rep met, they became more and more intrigued by what could be accomplished. They wrote up their plan of action and circulated it among council and staff members. The stage was set and the players assembled — twenty-five in all, twelve council and twelve staff, plus the pastor, who was a member of both groups.

Identifying Values

The session was scheduled to begin at nine on Saturday morning and end at noon. It started with prayer, using the theme of Pentecost, when the disciples were sent out to spread the Good News to all nations. Everyone had been asked to bring a Bible — extras were available for those who needed them. The first step was to look through the Bible and find a passage that suggested a core value, something that was essential to the life and mission of the parish.

After some time for quiet reflection, people counted off to form five groups of five each in order to share a scripture passage that struck them and what parish values it revealed. The planning committee had located a parishioner to act as a facilitator for the morning so that none of the council or staff had to worry about keeping the meeting on track. The facilitator got the people into groups and gave them instructions. Each person was to read a short section of the Bible passage and then say what it revealed to them about a particular value or aspect of the parish. Everyone took a turn while one group member listed the values on large sheets of newsprint. A surprising result of this process was that not only did people identify similar values, but in one group two people had chosen the exact same passage from the Bible. As one person said afterward, "It was scary. It felt as though the Spirit was right there in our midst, selecting the passage for us."

After thirty minutes, all returned to the large group to share what they had written down on the newsprint. Many values were common to more than one group. These included: "vibrant, participative liturgies," "lifelong growth in faith, cradle to grave," "reaching out to the poor and needy," "Eucharist as central," "a focus on Christ in our midst." Other values came from only one group but were acknowledged and supported by all. "Why didn't we think of that?" people said to one another as each group gave its report. Examples of these offerings included, "welcoming the stranger in our midst," "working together in partnership," "sharing our riches, talents, and treasure with others," "reaching out to those unlike ourselves," "a single parish of many hues and colors, ages and backgrounds."

From the five newsprints the facilitator constructed a single list of core values that all agreed were the most important. The effort spent on constructing this common list was worth the time it took, especially for what followed.

Forming a Statement

The council and staff agreed that the current parish mission statement was too long and it missed some of the core values that surfaced in the small groups. What was needed was a pithy, easy-to-remember statement that highlighted the role and purpose of the parish. For the rest of the morning the staff and council set about writing a new mission statement.

The pastor gave a brief explanation of what a mission statement should include. "It should answer these questions: Who are we as a parish? What is the function of the parish, which is to say, why are we here? How do we fulfill our purpose, and for whom does the parish exist?" He went on to add, "The answer to these questions should be contained in three or four lines at the most."

A few of the council members had brought along samples of good mission statements from their businesses to show everyone how much could be said in just a few sentences. The facilitator then passed out three-by-five-inch index cards and asked everyone to write down a short statement based on the combined list of core values they had before them. The index cards emphasized that the mission statement should be short and to the point.

Each individual worked at coming up with a sample statement, and then everyone returned to the same small groups they had met with previously. "The task," the facilitator explained, "is to listen to each person's statement. Then select the one you want to use as a framework or skeleton. Using that as a guide, add or sub-tract words and phrases, using ideas uncovered from other people's statements."

As group members listened to each other's statements it became apparent how each articulated the core values, although expressed in a variety of ways and styles. There was much similarity between them, but it was obvious that some were better crafted than others.

After thirty minutes of intense effort, each small group returned to the large gathering with their rendition of a new mission state-ment. As the small group statements were presented it became apparent that more time would be needed to blend the five into one, even in draft form. It was almost time to adjourn the meet-ing; lunch was waiting for them. The facilitator asked whether one person from each of the small groups would be willing to form an ad hoc writing committee that could come up with a single draft from the five statements.

Individuals agreed to join the ad hoc committee, and the council and staff made a commitment to return in a month so they could agree on a final form. Everyone was pleased with how much had been accomplished during the morning and were looking forward to celebrating a lunch together. That was until one of the staff members asked, "Haven't we forgotten something? We can't come up with a new mission statement without asking for people's feedback and reactions. This might be a good opportunity to raise interest among the parishioners about what we stand for and what is special about this parish. Also, how do we know that others feel the same way we do about the mission and purpose of our parish?"

"Good thinking," the pastor interjected. "Suppose we wait to see what the committee comes up with over the month. When we come together we'll settle on a working draft that can go to the leaders and people for their suggestions and ideas. In the meantime, everyone start thinking about how we could plan and organize this feedback process. This could be a marvelous 'event' in the life of the parish."

People clapped in affirmation of the pastor's suggestion. They began looking forward to their next gathering to see what the draft might look like and to plan ways for getting reactions from the parishioners. The pastor then asked Jan to lead the group in saying grace. "After all, Jan, it was your question that got us started with all this creative thinking and productive activity."

Questions

1. What are a few core values that make your parish or group unique and special?

2. How does your mission statement incorporate these values, or if not, how could a new one be formulated?

Chapter Five

Mission Awareness

A mission statement is only as good as how well it is known and put into use, especially in shaping parish structures, goals, and decision making. In the last chapter, the pastor, staff, and council had come together to draft a new articulation of what they felt were the core values of the parish, what made it unique and special as a reflection of Gospel values in the Catholic tradition. But did the parishioners as a whole share their views and opinions?

Taking It to the People

The select committee whose task it was to draft a single statement from the five versions coming out of the Saturday workshop finished its work in record time. Committee members were pleased with the result and circulated the draft to staff and council members via email. The response that came back was very positive. The new statement was well focused, easy to remember, and a good description of what were essential aspects of the parish.

The next step was to get reactions from other parish leaders and ministers, those most active in parish activities and programs. The drafting committee emailed the statement to the heads of every group and ministry in the parish, asking them to take it to the next meeting of their organization or committee in order to find out what people thought of it. This took a month to accomplish because most parish groups met only once a month. The feedback was affirming and enthusiastic with only a few suggested changes. As one chairperson said of her group's discussion, "We finally know what we stand for as a parish. This will be a great guide and reference for us as we plan our year's activities and projects."

Step 3 was to take it to the parishioners, those who attended the weekend liturgies, as well as those who were not active members of the parish. A weekend in October was chosen for this feedback. The draft of the new statement was printed on cards and put in the pews for all the Masses, along with instructions to make any changes or adaptations people thought necessary. There was also blank space at the bottom of the card where individuals could indicate what the statement meant to them or what it implied about important aspects or characteristics of the parish. The celebrant at each Mass used the draft as the basis for the homily. This was followed by a member of the pastoral council who explained to the congregation the reaction process.

People were invited to reflect on the draft statement by answering this question, "In what ways does this reflect what you believe the parish to be?" They were to write comments and reactions to this question on the back of the index card. The draft statement was then used as an alternative to the Creed so that the entire congregation recited the statement out loud. The ushers then collected the reaction cards as they took up the collection.

This was a good process for those attending church, but it did not include the parishioners who didn't come to Mass that weekend. How would they be able to offer their wisdom about the statement? One of the staff members suggested that a special mailing be sent out to all registered parishioners, including a letter of explanation signed by the pastor, staff, and council; the response card; and a return envelope. It took some effort to get all of the staff's and council's signatures on the letter, but the leadership felt this was an important mailing and that it deserved a special emphasis. It was a costly endeavor to send this to everyone, and some of the staff members suspected that only a few people would respond, but the pastor wanted to make sure all were invited to participate.

More than expected did return the envelopes with their feedback. Many of the response cards began by thanking the leadership for asking their opinion. Once again, the responses were very positive and affirmed the effort to articulate the unique character and purpose of the parish.

The drafting committee, along with extra help from staff and council members, went through the reaction cards looking for significant suggestions and adaptations to the statement. Surprisingly almost everyone liked what it contained, many offering implications and insights prompted by the statement as well. For instance, one person said, "This statement speaks strongly about being an open and welcoming community. We should put up a huge banner outside of church that reads, 'Strangers Welcomed!' And if that is what we profess, we had better get down to putting it into practice." Another remarked, "This statement is the first time I've had any idea what we are about as a parish. I've been coming here for over twenty years, and finally I know what we stand for." A third wrote, "It says in the statement that we are sent out to spread the Good News. We had better believe in this Good News enough to invite others to join us. We are so timid about our faith. It's time we let others in on this great secret of Christ's life within us and in our church."

The staff and council reassembled for a follow-up meeting a few weeks after getting reactions from the parishioners. They could not believe all that had transpired over recent months. New life and excitement were stirring in the parish as active and inactive members alike reflected on the mission and purpose of the parish. At the conclusion of this meeting the pastor, staff, and council participated in a ritual signing of the new mission statement. One person was chosen to write the agreed-upon final draft on a large posterboard and, as meditative music played in the background, each individual came forward to add his or her signature. The posterboard was then placed on a table, and all joined hands in a circle around the statement and slowly read it aloud together. This is what they said:

> *Our mission is:*
>
> **to welcome** *all to join us around the table of the Eucharist,*
>
> **to prepare** *one another for living the Catholic faith in our daily lives,*
>
> **to send** *each other out to act justly, serve others, and spread the Good News of Jesus Christ.*[3]

Getting the Statement "Out There"

As mentioned earlier, a mission statement is only as good as how well it is known and put into use by the leaders and parishioners. This is the challenge of any statement of purpose no matter how descriptive and well crafted. After all the work put into this statement, the staff and council wanted to make sure it became an active and living presence in the parish, something everyone knew, could recite from memory, and would use for shaping the future direction of parish ministries and programs. How to do this?

"We have asked parishioners for their feedback," the pastor declared at a council meeting. "Let's go to them again for ideas about how to make it alive and visible in the parish community."

"How about a special town hall meeting as a gathering of the entire parish to brainstorm ideas?" a council member suggested.

"Great idea," the council chairperson piped up. "But we have to do it quickly as a way of ratifying the new statement in the parish community, just as we have done here among ourselves. How soon could we plan it and get people to come? Could we do it within a month, do you suppose?"

"Yes!" came back the response from all the council members. And so it was. With the help of the staff, a special task group was formed to plan the agenda and run the town hall meeting. Others volunteered to coordinate the publicity. They wanted this to be "an event" that the parish could celebrate as a whole and look back on as a turning point for the community.

A special effort was made to have the heads of every parish group and organization personally invite their membership to attend. The original goal was to get two hundred people to attend, but the task group decided to think big and expect twice that number. It was a good thing that it did because almost three hundred people showed up, both "the regulars" and infrequent Mass-goers alike.

The first item on the agenda was to use the new statement as the opening prayer. The assembly was grouped into three large sections. After an initial welcome by the pastor and an opening song, each section was asked to pray quietly for a few moments on one of three words from the statement, either "welcome," "prepare," or "send."

The pastor began the prayer by stating, "Our mission is . . . " Then he paused so that the first third of the assembly could speak in unison, with as much feeling and energy as they could muster, "*to welcome all.*" Then a lector continued, "to join us around the table of the Eucharist." After this the second section chanted, "*to prepare one another,*" and a catechist in the religious education program followed up with, "for living the Catholic faith in our daily lives." Finally, the last third chimed in with, "*to send each other out,*" and a member of the St. Vincent de Paul Society concluded with "to act justly, serve others, and spread the Good News of Jesus Christ." The entire gathering responded with a resounding "Amen!"

Everyone had been given a copy of the mission statement as they entered. It was the size of a credit card so that people could put it in their billfolds, purses, or wallets. Using this as an example, the organizers asked everyone to spend a moment quietly thinking about other ways this statement could be made known and used in the parish. Each individual was given an index card for this personal reflection. The reflection card also contained a number from one to forty. The next step was to break into groups of seven or eight, each with a recorder, as a way of sharing people's insights and ideas.

The discussions were lively as each small group explored ways to keep the mission statement alive and active in the minds and hearts of the parishioners. Some of the more creative suggestions included:

1. Putting the three key words from the statement on banners attached to the light posts leading up the road to the parish so that people could walk past "welcome," "prepare," and "send" as they came to church.

2. Making up magnets for people's refrigerators and computers that had the statement on it in the same size as the credit card passed out at the Town Hall.

3. Reading the statement at all the Masses once a month, splitting it up so that the first part is read at the beginning, the middle section at the petitions, and the last segment after the final blessing.

4. Putting the statement on the homepage of the parish website, on the front of the bulletin, and on the back of parish envelopes so that it is the first thing people see.

5. Encouraging a songwriting contest to put the statement to music, with the best three versions premiered on the parish feast day. All the parishioners would have a chance to vote for their favorite song, and this could be used for years to come as the "Parish Anthem."

6. Preparing special nametags that have the mission statement printed around the blank space where people put their names.

7. From the first Sunday of Lent to Pentecost Sunday, starting every parish meeting with the words, "How does what we are going to do at this meeting reflect the intent and purpose

of our mission statement?" Then, at the conclusion of the meeting, the statement is read in unison as the concluding prayer.

8. Displaying the mission statement on a large screen during the annual parish festival, with streamers throughout the area with the words "welcome," "prepare," "sent" repeated again and again.

9. Setting aside a special "Mission Weekend" each year where the statement is celebrated and re-ratified, along with a "State of the Parish" report from the pastoral council. There could also be a special multimedia presentation by various parish groups and ministries that described what they had done during the year to put the parish mission statement into practice.

10. Whenever a major decision is made in the parish, beginning the deliberations with a reading of the mission statement so that whatever decision is made flows out of the values contained in the statement.

11. Putting together a video presentation that describes how the statement was fashioned and what a difference it has made to the life and energy of the parish. This could be shown to newcomers, as well as to other parishes that might like to learn from the experience.

Conclusion

Section One of this book is entitled "Experiencing Covenant: What Drives Us?" It began with the importance that each and every individual possesses for effecting change in the parish. It only takes one person, a risk-taker, to move the parish in a new direction. Next comes a reflection on what a parish is all about. Why is it necessary, and what does it have to offer that can't be found anywhere else? From this reflection comes an emphasis on mission, feeling the call to make a difference, responding to the urge to move from theory into practice. This is a deep, inner feeling that gains acceptance as others join the effort. To make this feeling concrete and operative, it needs expression and articulation. This is called the group's purpose or mission statement. It is not a long list of platitudes but an active, rousing, pithy definition of what is essential and unique about the parish, or any group, for that matter.

Once articulated, the mission statement must be blazoned in the hearts and minds of those who call themselves part of the group. The statement is not just on a plaque hanging up somewhere or listed on parish stationery; it must have power and authority. It should direct all else that happens in the parish. It is the turning point for any organization, a declaration of what it stands for, something that is well known and lived out by all who belong to the group, whether it be a parish, organization, movement, or ministry.

Questions

1. In what ways does your mission statement have power and authority to influence all that happens in the parish — or if it does not, how could it?

2. In what ways could your parish mission statement become better known among the parishioners, both the active and inactive members?

Section Two

Putting the Pieces Together

In Christ the whole structure is joined together
and grows into a holy temple in the Lord;
in whom you also are built together spiritually
into a dwelling place for God.

— Ephesians 2:21–22

Every good mission needs a structure to hang on, a network of relationships that allows the purpose of the group to find expression and articulation. It does no good to have every individual and group know what is essential and unique about the parish if there are no predictable patterns and organizational structures for putting the mission into operation. Fitting all the pieces together is a critical aspect of a well-functioning parish community. The chapters that follow will deal with the various aspects of parish structures, beginning with the pastor and moving through the important co-ordinating groups of staff, council, commissions, committees, and ministerial groupings.

Chapter Six

The Simplest of Structures
Two Better Than One

The first chapter of *The Parish as Covenant* suggested a change of system in which the pastor is no longer at the center of the parish circle so that not everything that happens in the parish depends upon him.[4] This is a pastoring structure that has a dual focus, two people sharing the leadership together as partners. There are many variations of this dual-focus partnership currently operating in parishes, some with one other person sharing the load with the pastor and, in other places, two persons working with the pastor in providing direction and leadership to the parish community.

Pastor as Key

When people ask us what is the greatest shift or change that happens as a result of our involvement in a parish, we respond, "The pastor!" It is up to him, as the canonical head of the parish, to choose to enter into a dual focus of shared leadership. The shift must be real and not just a rhetorical experience of going through the motions.

One pastor who wanted to use our services had a reputation for being a micro-manager. Everything, and that meant *everything*, went through his office, from major decisions to the smallest and pickiest of details. When he asked for our help, we confronted him with this information. He denied it, but to his credit, he checked it out with his staff. "Am I a micro-manager, whatever that is?" he asked. One courageous staff person, the deacon, who was not dependent upon a parish salary, spoke up. "Yes, as a matter of fact, you are. And here are a few examples just from last week." The deacon rattled off a list of decisions the pastor had made on his own. The pastor looked around at the staff and sensed their muted agreement. "Okay, I give in. I'm willing to give this a chance. I have no idea where this will lead, but let's call in these 'outsiders' and see where it will take us."

That was the beginning of a change, both in the pastor and in the parish, one that has lasted for more than five years. Everything was possible because the pastor was open to a change. During the course of our work with the parish, the pastor, along with a search committee, made up a job description for a new position, a parish administrator. This person would work as an equal partner with the pastor, with clear separation of roles and responsibilities. As a whole, the pastor would handle the pastoral, sacramental, and spiritual side of the parish. The new administrator would be responsible for moderating the staff and dealing with personnel issues, overseeing parish finances, both income and expenses, coordinating the upkeep of parish buildings and grounds, and handling other administrative duties, including emergencies, security issues, and physical breakdowns. The pastor was skeptical that anyone could be found to match this description. "And on top of all that," he added, "this administrator will have to deal with me and keep me from putting my nose into everything. That's a full-time job in itself."

But a person was found, a young Hispanic man from another parish who had had experience working in a collaborative setting with a pastor just recently retired. "I need a new challenge," he said when applying for the job. "I'm in a rut, and this will give me a fresh start. I'm not too sure the new pastor in my present place is that open to having me as partner. It's not everyone's cup of tea."

He applied and was chosen for the position. The fit was right, the chemistry between pastor and new administrator matched — a most important ingredient for a dual focus. The pastor trusted him, and he, in turn, respected the pastor for all his gifts and for his willingness and determination to change. From the beginning of their interaction they provided a model of collaborative leadership to the staff, leaders, and parish community.

Such a perfect fit is not common. Usually it takes time, sometimes up to a year, before a permanent arrangement is in place. When we work with parishes, we suggest starting with a temporary position for an administrator, perhaps six months in duration, and let it be a part-time commitment of fifteen to twenty hours a week. Look within the parish for someone who might fit this description of administrator/parish manager/personnel director in order to get this partnership with the pastor started.

In one parish the term of office was over for the head of the finance committee. The man was a retired executive with extensive experience in personnel management. He was also a sensitive and prayerful person, characteristics that are always an important part of the job description. We approached the gentleman with our idea. "Would you consider coming out of retirement for six months," we asked, "to work with the pastor as a parish administrator?"

"Oh, I don't know," was his reply. "My wife is not going to like this. Let me get back to you."

A week later, while having dinner at their home, his wife gave him her blessing. "I think this will be good for you, John. You like trying out something new, and this certainly will be a new adventure — for everyone involved."

The pastor was delighted because he trusted John and knew he filled up what was lacking in himself, especially dealing fairly but firmly with conflicts. "As you know," the pastor admitted, "whenever I see a conflict on the horizon, I'm on the next plane heading in the opposite direction."

One of the first tasks John had to handle was staff divisions and competition. Because the pastor was not able to confront conflicts, some members of the staff had abused their position, taking advantage of the poor system of accountability and oversight. Within two months, when staff members realized that doing end-runs around the administrator and complaining to the pastor did no good, a change in the staff culture began to take place. Office spaces were rearranged, meetings became more productive, effective use of time was encouraged, roles were clarified, accounting for one's time became a regular tradition — all done with gentle prodding and subtle pressure. The pastor was amazed at the shift; the parishioners themselves noticed the change. "This is a much happier place to work, thanks to you, John," the pastor volunteered at one of their weekly confabs. "Can't you just stay on for the rest of my tenure here?"

"Nope — better we get someone in here on a permanent basis. I'm just getting the position ready for your *real* partner. Now that you know what it feels like, we have to make sure the staff, leaders, and parishioners know this is not just a flash in the pan. This is a whole new way of operating. The culture of partnership is here to stay!"

A few months into his new job, John began to coordinate a search process for a permanent position, making sure money was budgeted for this purpose. Among all the candidates, the person who was eventually hired was a parishioner who had taken an early retirement. At the age of fifty-five he was more than willing to try out something new. John showed him the ropes, made sure the pastor would be comfortable with the new person, and then withdrew in order to resume being an "ordinary parishioner," one of many benefiting from this new dual-focus arrangement. Jim, the new administrator, was the right person for the job. He was happy that John had prepared the ground for him, bringing the staff from lone rangers to contented team-players, and the pastor from micromanaging to an awareness of a freedom he had never experienced before. He was now able to be the pastoral, spiritual leader for which he was trained and to which he was ordained.

In another parish, the right combination turned out to be not one other person in partnership with the pastor but *two* others. One of the threesome was astute at handling the administrative duties that included finances, building projects, and the coordination of the support staff. The other person of the trio was gifted in managing conflicts and personnel issues and as a result worked more with the pastoral staff. The pastor and the other two "partners" met on a regular basis, at least once a week, not only to communicate with each other and coordinate their efforts, but also to act as a resource to each other by offering one another feedback and suggestions about how to proceed with a problem or a particular situation.

In yet another parish that had a smaller staff, hiring an administrator was out of the question; there were no funds for such a position. The existing director of religious education for children and youth gave the job over to her competent assistant and took a new role on staff as part-time administrator and partner with the pastor. She also spent part of her time as the new adult enrichment director, an area she had always wanted to develop. This turned out to be an excellent arrangement for all involved. The definition of her role created a new level of interaction between herself and the pastor. He accepted her as an equal and as someone complementing his own position and function in the parish.

Each place has its own issues and its own unique climate and culture. The overarching task, however, is the same. Find a partner for the pastor as a way of taking him out of the bull's-eye and creating a dual focus of shared leadership and co-responsibility.

The Reluctant Pastor

Sometimes when people are introduced to this new partnership concept, they complain that "it will never work in our parish. The pastor would never consent to sharing his authority." Our response is, "Perhaps, but have you ever asked him about giving it a try?"

The position of being pastor in a modern parish, at least in the Catholic tradition, is an impossible one. He is required to be on top of everything, and then take on one or more additional parishes or missions besides. It is a dead end, one doomed to frustration and failure. The pastor, wanting to be present to the people, finds that just the opposite occurs. He rushes from one Mass to another in different locations with little chance to mingle or meet the parishioners. Having a partner or a dual-focus structure will not solve all the issues, but it does provide at least one other person who is on an equal footing with himself, someone who can give him feedback, hold him accountable, and help him maintain healthy boundaries between work and his personal life. And when the toilets overflow just before the entrance song for Mass, there is help at the other end of the cell phone.

Even for those pastors who are good managers and who thrive on keeping everything running smoothly, they know they can't do it alone. Having someone else to share the load and act as a confidant and wisdom figure brings out the best in any pastor, no matter how competent and gifted.

It does help, however, to have someone from outside the parish situation assist with this shift to a dual focus or partnership model. Sometimes an objective set of eyes and ears can discern what those in the middle of the situation miss. One pastor we worked with bought into the concept of finding a partner at the beginning of our engagement with the parish. He proudly brought in his prospective candidate for our reaction. After the person left he could see we were not impressed. The person he had in mind had not stopped talking throughout the entire interview. Listening, so important for a good administrator, did not appear to be his strong point. What this experience taught us was, "Don't jump at the first prospective candidate who comes along." Design a good search process and stick to it. Start with a temporary position lasting no more than six months and have a thorough review and assessment before having the person sign on for a longer commitment. It has to be the right person, one who frees up the pastor's role, not makes it worse by putting more strain and tension on the pastor's shoulders.

This is the simplest of parish structures, finding a partner for the pastor. But it has to be the right person (or persons) if the structure is going to work and if it is to become a model of collaborative partnership for the rest of the parish community.

Questions

1. What are the steps that would have to take place to move toward a dual focus of pastoral leadership?

2. What are the advantages and drawbacks for the pastor to have one or two persons to act as partners with him in providing leadership and direction in the parish?

Chapter Seven

Structures for a More Effective Staff

Ours is a theology of partnership. Jesus sent his followers out two-by-two to heal the sick and spread the Good News (Mark 6:7). St. Paul speaks of us as being "co-workers with the Lord" (1 Cor. 3:9). This is the letter that describes Paul as doing the planting and Apollos the watering, but God is the One who makes the seed grow. We are co-workers with God and with one another. In practical terms this means establishing a culture of partnership throughout the parish, beginning with the pastor and staff. The last chapter described how the pastor might form a covenant with one or two other persons in leading, directing, and maintaining the parish. This chapter is devoted to the structure of the staff, how staff members might team up with one another and with other parish leaders in doing their ministry. God is in the dialogue between individuals and groups, which is to say, God is in the partnership and in the covenant they make with one another. The result of this dialogue and sharing is something more than any one person could do alone.

Another name for this is to call it a "theology of relinquishment." What this requires is that those in authority let go of the controls and share power and decision making with others. The pastor is willing to work with an administrator or pastoral associate so that each has a sphere of influence and an area of ministry to handle. So, too, with staff members. If they are willing to let go of doing all the planning and deciding by themselves, allowing others to share in shaping the ministry, project, or program, then they are practicing a theology of letting go, of relinquishment.

Consider the liturgy director. As he prepares for a new academic year he thinks to himself, "I'm going to try out something different this time around. It's not going to be all my own show anymore. After all, it's not my liturgy; it doesn't belong to me."

He begins with the choir director. "Julie, we have worked side by side for some time now but not really together. You handle the music, and I organize the liturgies. Let's try out something new. Could we sit down and plan *together* what we want to do for Advent? I'll also be working with the liturgy planning committee on this. But just for now, you and I, how could we make this more of a shared experience this coming year?"

Amazed and delighted, the choir director readily agreed. She had always felt left out of the planning and somewhat on the edge of the liturgical planning process. When they found a time to sit down and discuss various options and possibilities, the liturgy director began by saying, "I know your area is the choir, but you must have many ideas about the liturgies as a whole. How could we do it better?"

The result of this invitation and consequent dialogue was not only many new ideas for Advent, but a new mutuality between the two of them that had never been there before. The choir was no longer a separate entity added to the planning of the week-end Masses at the end of the process. Instead, as a result of this new partnership, the music became more of an integral part of the theme and direction of the liturgies. Not only that, the level of congregational singing improved because those in charge of the music felt more ownership and energy to make the Masses better.

Encouraged by the success of this new way of proceeding, the liturgy director decided to do the same with the liturgy planning committee. Up to this point he had been leading the committee himself. No more. He called in the most experienced member of the group and asked if she would be willing to work with him in directing the committee.

"We can be co-chairs together, or better yet, you be the chair and I'll be your back-up and resource person. We can work out the agenda for the meetings together and assess afterward how well it went and what we could do better. The planning of liturgies, after all, belongs to the people, not to me."

The director was pleased at how well the new chair caught on to her task, and he found her to be a master at her job, bringing more life and involvement to the committee than he was able to do himself. No longer did the group look to him as the expert. They did their own reading and research, coming to the meetings with more awareness and expertise. As one person put it, "We are here to take our liturgies to a new level of praise, celebration, and communal worship not known before in our parish."

In another example, this same emphasis on partnership might lead a director of religious formation to link up with the school principal or the youth minister so they can share with one another ideas and insights, discovering between them areas for mutual planning and development. This same director might also locate a "master catechist" from among the volunteer teachers and work with this person in shaping the formation programs for the coming year.

The pastoral associate in charge of outreach to the sick and homebound might find a nurse or some other qualified person in the parish who would be willing to work with her as a partner not only in caring for the sick but in exploring new programs that could help people deal with loss, limitations, and diminishment.[5] The possibilities become more apparent when a new culture of partnership and a theology of relinquishment are embraced by the staff.

One of the best ways to get started in this direction is to create "prayer partners" among staff members. Each month everyone pairs up with one other person on staff to talk over their ministry, share ideas, and pray for each other's cares and concerns. They might even pray together if they find this convenient and to their liking. This forms a spiritual bond between staff members, pastor included.

A Structure for Large Staffs

If the staff is under ten people, including both pastoral and support staff, then there is little need for any more of a structure than a weekly meeting together and pairing up with one another as prayer partners or for sharing ideas on ministry. When the staff grows larger so that there are at least ten people on the pastoral staff besides others who lend them support as secretaries, receptionists, bookkeepers, or managers of maintenance, then a more creative model of interaction might be necessary.

One structure that has worked well in parishes is to cluster all the staff into three groupings covering the areas of worship, formation, and administration, with one core staff member as the link and liaison with each cluster. There might also be a staff person overseeing community life and directing such areas as volunteer management, parish social functions, and hospitality. Ordinarily there is but one person covering this area without any support staff. The same might be true for outreach ministries, such as pastoral care, Christian service, peace and justice, or reaching out to inactive parishioners. Staff members in each of these two areas would be part of the core staff and not have a cluster of other staff members with whom to relate.

As a result of the reorganization, the "core staff" would include five individuals, each overseeing one of the five ministerial areas: worship, community life, formation, outreach, and administration. Add to this the pastor, and the core staff amounts to six people in all. This group would meet on a weekly basis. Three of the core staff would also coordinate a cluster of other staff members associated with worship, formation, or administration.

Parish Staff

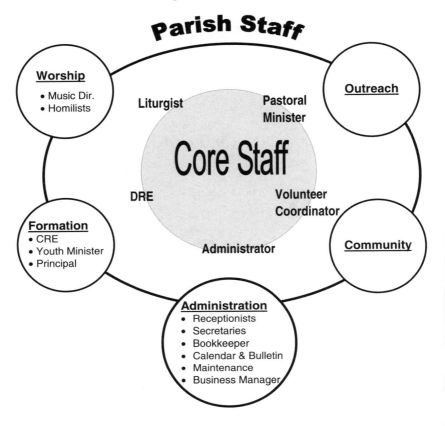

The worship area might include the priests and deacons, the liturgy director, those in charge of music, and any support staff linked to worship and liturgy. This worship cluster of staff would meet once or twice a month depending on the need. Some of its agenda items might include reflections on the weekend scripture readings as a help to those preparing homilies, suggestions for the liturgy planning committee or worship commission, and ways to foster an atmosphere of prayer, devotion, and spiritual reflection in the parish.[6]

A second cluster of staff members might include all those related to education and faith formation, including the principal (if there is a parish school), the director of religious formation, the youth minister, those in charge of the RCIA program or sacramental preparation, as well as all support staff associated with these ministries.

The third cluster would be administration, including those connected with finances, maintenance, stewardship, and administration. Each of the three clusters would meet on its own at least once a month to handle issues and concerns related to a particular area of ministry and to explore creative ways for improving their service ministry, either to the parishioners or beyond the parish membership. A diagram of this large staff structure might look like the diagram on the facing page.

In order to bond together as a total staff, a common meeting of all the pastoral staff and support staff would take place once a month, while the core staff would meet each of the other weeks during the month. These meetings need not last long because much of the business can be dealt with in the smaller groupings of the staff. The three clusters of worship, formation, and administration would meet on their own once or twice during the month.

Structuring Staff Meetings

Reporting is the bane of any meeting, especially staff meetings. Going around the group so all can share what they have been doing takes everyone else off the hook. All they have to do is listen but not do anything about it. A more productive model is one in which people are actively engaged in deciding, planning, and giving feedback. One way this can be accomplished, and with minimal preparation beforehand and no writing of minutes afterward, is described below.

In preparation for this new way of operating, the staff discerns three teams, those who have the talent for leading meetings, those who are gifted at leading prayer, and those who are good at taking notes. Once this is determined, then a leader, prayer person, and note-taker volunteer for the first meeting, using the format described below. An "agenda sheet" is kept in a central location throughout the week or made available on a computer network for staff members to list agenda items before the meeting. When people list an item, they also add their names or initials, as well as indicating what type of item it is. A sample agenda sheet is shown on the following page.

Whether it is the core staff meeting that happens once a week or the monthly meeting of the total staff, the time together need not last long because much of the business can be dealt with in the smaller groupings of the staff. When it is time for the meeting to take place, copies of the filled-out agenda sheet are made available for all those present. The prayer leader begins with a reflection, song, or meditation lasting four to seven minutes. Then the one leading the meeting invites people to do a quick "round robin" so people can indicate their frame of mind or share a brief personal story that would be of interest to all. This, too, takes from four to seven minutes. Some staffs use this time for a "weather report," that is, what is the climate like inside? Is it cloudy, sunny, rainy, stormy, in the middle of a whirlwind, or just a quiet breeze? This brief sharing gets everyone in tune with people's moods so they can be more understanding and accepting of what others may be going through at the moment.

Next comes the agenda items. First up are those items that have a check in the Information column. Perhaps number 3, 7, 12, and 15 have checks in this first column. Each one is taken in turn while the recorder makes notes on the right side of the agenda sheet. Others might add notes of their own to their own agenda sheet as well. There is little or no discussion connected with information items. These might include upcoming events to put on people's calendars; announcements about those who are sick, have died, or need extra prayers; and other key events that will affect the staff or other parish groups. If someone other than the person who checked the Information box wants to add feedback, or talk about the item, then the leader asks whether it involves a decision, feedback, or

AGENDA FOR STAFF MEETING

Chairperson _____ Date _____

   A. Prayer Leader: _____

   B. Sharing of personal reactions or experiences since the last meeting (4–7 minutes)

   C. Agenda items taken according to each category in turn.

   D. Summary of results at the end of the meeting.

   E. Evaluation of the meeting and the level of staff interaction.

Agenda Item	Member	I	D	F	P	N	Notes
1.							
2.							
3.							
4.							
5.							
6.							
7.							
8.							
9.							
10.							
11.							
12.							

Code Description:

   I Information: announcements, meeting dates, events (no discussion necessary)

   D Decision: items that have been discussed previously but now need a decision

   F Feedback: affirming or giving reactions to an existing program, event, ministry, etc.

   P Planning: needs discussion about an upcoming event, issue, problem, etc.

   N New Business: new issues included as time permits or put off for the next meeting planning and then adds a check in the appropriate column, along with the person's name who brought it up, saying, "Good. We'll get back to that later, but let's go on with the rest of the information items first."

After all of the information items have been covered, and this can usually be done quickly because there is little or no discussion, then the leader goes on to the **Decisions** column, calling on the person who checked the first decision item to lead the discussion. If there is one or another item that has some urgency to it and has to be handled first, then the item gets an asterisk instead of a check and is taken first before all other checks in the column.

The third column is for **Feedback**. Here staff members can offer one another support and affirmation for an event or ministry that took place since the last meeting. Others may want to offer suggestions and helps to another staff person, always with kindness and positive intent. As the staff learns how to give constructive feedback to one another, this increases trust and support among the staff as a whole.

The fourth column is for **Planning** items. These are topics that need some thought and discussion, although decisions on these matters may be taken up at a future meeting after people have had time to reflect on the matter. Finally, the **New Business** column is for those items that are added to the agenda and are included if time permits. If not, then they are put off until a future meeting.

The leader proceeds through all the checks, taking each column in turn. At the end, the person asks the recorder to highlight a few of the action items so that everyone is made aware of what was decided or what needs implementation before the next meeting. Finally the leader asks, "How did it go today? Is there anything we could do to make the next meeting better?" This brief assessment is critical to making future meetings effective and enjoyable to all who attend. A new leader, prayer person, and note-taker are then determined for the next meeting. The note-taker for the current meeting then makes copies of the "official version" of the agenda sheet immediately after the meeting, putting it in people's boxes or sending it around by email so that everyone has a copy, both those who were present at the meeting and those who were absent.

A staff meeting structured in this way should last no more than an hour or an hour and a half. The same format can be used for the weekly core staff meeting, the various staff cluster meetings throughout the month, and the one large gathering of the total staff each month.[7]

Questions

1. How is the current staff structured and how productive are its meetings?

2. What changes might be needed so that the staff is more effective in its work and is sharing the planning and decision making with others?

Chapter Eight

Structuring for Ownership

The theme of this book is joint ownership of the parish shared by pastor, staff, leaders, and people. They are co-workers and are in partnership with God and one another. It is a covenantal relationship, everyone working out of a common mission together. Establishing a structure of joint ownership is the key to this covenant becoming a reality. The structure need not be complex or confounding. Begin simply with the formation of coordinating, visioning groups in each of the five key areas of parish life: worship, community life, formation, outreach, and administration. These oversight groups are often called "commissions" to distinguish them from committees, task groups, or ministries that are subgroups associated with an area of parish life.

Each commission is made up of six to nine members chosen from those active in a ministry, group, or organization connected to one of the five areas. Suppose, for instance, that you are a choir member of the 10:30 a.m. Sunday liturgy. You have been a faithful singer for the last five years. Someone from the parish calls you and invites you to an organizational meeting for the formation of a new worship commission. "This will be one of five commissions," the caller explains. "We are just getting started with a new way of structuring the parish. We thought you would be a good person to be part of this group. It will be overseeing the whole liturgical, prayer, and devotional side of the parish. You have a good sense of vision and can see the bigger picture. That's why we are asking you to come to this meeting."

Flattered to be asked, you agree to attend the first meeting, mostly out of curiosity to see what this new way of organizing the parish might be. Once there, you end up being chosen as one of nine people on a provisional worship commission. You are assured that this is just to get the new structure "off the ground," as the pastor put it. It will be a six-month commitment with a chance to continue on the commission if all works out well.

"What did I get myself into?" you keep saying to yourself on your way home. "I don't have time for this. But it was nice to be asked, and this new setup of the five commissions does look intriguing."

The first gathering of the five new commissions is an orientation meeting. The second Tuesday of each month for the next six months is designated as the "Leadership Night." The night would begin with prayer, each commission taking a turn leading it. After a few minutes for announcements, the commissions would meet on their own for an hour. At the end of that time, each commission would give a two-minute report of its work, followed by a social. Once again, the commissions would take turns providing refreshments for the evening. One staff person would act as a resource to each commission. For instance, the worship commission, the one you belong to, would have the liturgy/music director as its resource, someone you know well from singing in the choir.

At the first Leadership Night, one of the first tasks for each commission is to discern from among its members two people to serve as the co-chairs of the group. To your great amazement, you are chosen to fill that post in the worship commission, along with an older person who is a longtime lector. Because you don't have to do it all alone, you consent to give it a try. "I can't do too much harm in just six months," you jokingly announce to the group who picked you.

After the hour is up, your co-chair gives a report to the entire gathering, making sure to stay within the two-minute limit. During the social you meet with your new partner and the liturgy director to arrange a time for working up an agenda for next month's meeting. "Some of the tasks," the staff resource mentions, "include identifying all the groups and ministries associated with worship, assigning commission members to connect with the heads of those groups, and then trying to figure out the general state of worship and liturgy in the parish as a whole. It is up to the commission to find out what is working well and what needs a little help. This might give us an idea of what we will need to work on in the future."

Before the next gathering of the commissions, you and your co-chair, with the help of the liturgy director, work up an agenda for the meeting. This is sent out to all the other worship commission members so they can see it before the meeting. Forty-five people arrive at the next Leadership Night ready to get down to the business of coordinating and overseeing all that is going on in the parish, not just in worship but in community life, formation, outreach, and administration as well. Everyone seems excited about the prospect of making a difference in the parish. They welcome the new structure and are ready to do whatever it takes to put it into operation.

For the hour that the nine members of the worship commission meet, all of the ministries and groups connected to worship are identified and then split up so that each person has one or two groups to connect with over the next thirty days. They are to ask two questions of those in charge of a particular ministry: What is going well in your ministry or group? Tell us so we can celebrate your successes with you. What needs help or what could be done better or with greater effectiveness?

The time remaining in the one-hour meeting is spent exploring possible goals to work on over the next few months. One person suggests that more could be done to welcome people into the liturgies. "Everyone — young or old, longtime parishioners or newcomers," she explains, "should be invited to join in with the Mass."

Although many other ideas surface during the discussion, this effort at greater hospitality becomes the most popular and is chosen as a possible goal to work on over the next six months.

At the end of the meeting you ask, "How could we make our time together better next month?"

"Keep the meetings as productive as this one," a young woman comments. Another speaks up, "And no reports, please. We can give each other memos of whatever we need to know. Let's keep our time together productive and get things accomplished." A third person adds, "I want to leave here each month with something to show for our time together. So far, so good. Keep it interesting and enjoyable, and I'll keep coming back."

As a result of these suggestions, you and your co-chair make sure that the next meeting does not have lengthy reports about the information collected from the various liturgical groups and ministries. Instead you make it a quick "go-around" about the state of what's going on. One discovery is that the Eucharistic ministers need better coordination and scheduling. Another is that the servers need more instruction and direction. A third is the need for the ushers to come together so they can be informed about a possible new emphasis on hospitality and welcoming. This last need leads to a discussion about how to get a new "greeters ministry" off the ground. "It's not our job to do it," the staff resource person explains. "We should probably put together a special hospitality committee to organize it and get it into operation."

Role of the Commission

The above example of how to get a commission structure started and what some of its tasks might be can be summed up in the four functions of a parish commission: *link, assess, vision,* and *funnel.* All it takes to initiate such a structure is to call together five ad hoc groups of nine members apiece, each with a staff person acting as a resource but not being in charge or the chairperson of the group. Then choose two people to act as co-chairs and give the commission six months to get started.

During the six-month interval, each program, project, organization, ministry, or group is identified and connected to one of the commissions. All members of a commission are assigned one or more groups to *link* with and act as a connector to those subgroups. Making these contacts each month will uncover areas that may need support, help, or accountability. For instance, in the example mentioned above, the ushers had never met together as a group. They needed to have a discussion about greeters being assigned to the weekend liturgies. Although not much had been done to greet people as they entered church each weekend, the ushers still needed a chance to talk with one another and with the new hospitality committee to learn and become comfortable with what changes and adaptations might be required of them.

The second task for a commission, along with linking, is to *assess* what is happening with each ministry, group, or committee, always looking for areas that might need some help, support, or assistance. Once identified, these areas of need become future agenda items for the commission. It might invite people from a particular ministry or group to attend a commission meeting and talk about what they are doing and how they could improve. One or more commission members might visit with those in charge of the group to see how the commission could offer support or assistance. Assessing might also include holding groups or individuals accountable for what they said they would accomplish within a given time frame.

A third important task for the commission is *visioning*. What could worship, for instance, look like if everything went right? In the previous example, an initial dream or desire was to have greeters at every door of the church for every weekend Mass. This is a realizable goal that fulfilled the mission statement mentioned in chapter 5, "to welcome all to join us around the table of the Eucharist...."

But it is not up to the worship commission to organize the greeters. Its function is to *funnel* this task to a newly formed hospitality committee. The commission would define the role of this committee, find a few key people to spearhead this effort, uncover names of those who would be good committee members, and then give the committee the freedom to locate greeters, train them for this ministry, schedule them for the Masses, and hold them accountable for showing up. The worship commission would construct a timeline for when the hospitality committee needs to be up and running, and would arrange for progress reports from the committee every three to six months of its operation.

Essentials for a Commission

If a commission structure is to be successful, these four ingredients are essential:

1. *Staff resource person:* One of the nine people on a commission should be a member of the parish staff — but no more than one. If there are two or more staff persons present, the other members of the commission tend to pull back and let the staff do the planning and visioning. This one staff resource is a full and active participant of the commission but is not the one "in charge." Rather, the staff person acts as a resource, providing breadth, experience, and expertise to the commission's activity. As mentioned earlier, the staff resource person and the co-chairs connect before the meeting to draw up the agenda, which is then sent around to all the participants so they know what to expect and what to be thinking about in preparation for the meeting. The staff resource also meets with the co-chairs after the meeting to evaluate the effectiveness of the session and determine what might make it better next time.

The five staff resource persons, along with the pastor, make up the "core staff," as mentioned in chapter 7. One of the items for this weekly meeting of the core staff is a discussion of the commissions, which ones are doing well and which ones need greater support and resourcing. The addition of a staff resource person on the commission is critical to its operation and vitality. Although this staff resource is there only to help the group and not run the meeting, being a member of the group lends support and confidence to other members of the commission.

2. *Co-chairs:* "Keeping the Covenant" on the commission level involves joint leadership by two people rather than by a single chairperson. Discerning who these two people are is a crucial function of the commission at the start of each year's new term. Finding the right balance and complementarity of leadership can result in more effective and productive meetings. This provides a more enjoyable atmosphere for all those who attend. The way in which the meeting is conducted will vary with the unique talents and abilities of the co-chairs. One person might be gifted in conducting an efficient meeting, while the other is better at pulling everyone into the conversation. One person may be a good timekeeper, while the other chairperson knows when to let the discussion continue until a good solution is found. The separation of duties and tasks, in other words, will depend on the two people involved. They may take turns running the same meeting, or they may alternate months in taking the lead. One person may conduct all the meetings while the other interjects when one or another commission member is not being heard or takes over. The co-chairs might also take turns in leading the evaluation process at the end of the meeting or in getting a volunteer to give the two-minute report to the other commissions at the end of the evening. It is a complementary partnership, an agreement of mutual sharing by the two co-chairs, a prime example of covenantal leadership in which two individuals rather than a single person lead the group and keep it on track and productive.

3. *Common Leadership Night:* A third ingredient that helps the commission structure work well is to have all of the commissions meet at the same time and in the same place every month. This makes it possible for them to relate and communicate with each

other. It is important that this meeting happens on a monthly basis in order to keep the momentum alive and the work of the commissions present to all those involved. Coming together at the same time each month establishes a tradition to which people grow accustomed. It also becomes known in the parish that this one day of the month is the Leadership Night. Nothing else of note happens that night; no religious formation, no choir, no Christian service projects, no other event that draws a significant number of parishioners. This is the time the forty-five leaders involved in the oversight and planning of the parish come together to give direction to key aspects of parish life.

With careful preparation of the agenda beforehand and with well-directed facilitation and leadership, the hour set aside for the commission meeting each month can accomplish all that needs to be done to take the parish to the next level, whatever that might be. To make sure that the evening does stay on track, it helps to have a timekeeper or facilitator guiding the meeting, someone who is not a member of any of the commissions but keeps everything running smoothly. This is the person who holds all groups accountable and makes sure they stay within their agreed-upon timeline. This facilitator, in a gentle but firm manner, makes sure the meeting starts on time with the opening prayer and that the commissions begin their one-hour session fifteen minutes after the start of the meeting. As the hour draws to a close, the facilitator makes the rounds of the commissions, reminding them to bring closure to their deliberations and to have the two-minute report ready for the general assembly. When the reports are given, the facilitator makes sure the time limit is kept. If one report is allowed to go over the two minutes, this will be a signal to others that they can do the same. Keeping the reports to within two minutes keeps interest alive and the evening short.

A more subtle task of the facilitator is to pay attention to how well the commission meetings are going: observing whether all participants have a chance to contribute, that tasks are being accomplished in a timely manner, and that the business is being conducted in an enjoyable, involving atmosphere. If this is not happening in one or another of the commissions, the facilitator makes a note of this and shares these observations with the staff resource person or the co-chairs after the meeting.

4. *Covenant Booklet:* Every member of the commissions needs a reference to fall back on, a manual or guide that describes "this is how we operate, how we do things around here." This booklet functions not only as a leadership manual but as a description of the covenant that people make with one another as members of the commissions. The covenant booklet need not be long, some twenty to thirty pages in all. It might begin with the parish mission statement that is the basis and rationale for all that the parish does and hopes to accomplish. Each commission would have its own purpose statement spelled out in the booklet, defining its scope and range of activity. The booklet would list all the groups and ministries associated with each commission, a description of how decisions are made, how new members are chosen for the commissions, terms of office, and expectations for membership.[8]

The covenant booklet is a loose-leaf binder so that changes, additions, and deletions can be made as the need arises. The final page is a roster of membership. A typical term of office on a commission is three years, so that each year one-third of the membership rotates off and new people join the group. When this happens, those leaving the commissions sit down, one-on-one, with those coming on the commission, and together they go through the booklet as a training and orientation exercise. When they get to the last page, the one whose term is completed gives the booklet to the new person, who then signs the roster as an indication that now it is time to begin service as a member of the commission.

For the first few years of this new structure's existence it helps to do the training of new people with all of the commission members present. This serves as a refresher course for those already on the commission, as well as a training exercise for the new members.[9]

68

Questions

1. In your parish, who does the oversight and planning for each of the key areas of parish life?

2. What changes would have to take place so that all those in leadership positions are working well together and are connected with all of the ministries and organizations of the parish?

Chapter Nine

The Pastoral Council
Is the Glue

Where does the pastoral council fit into the commission structure spelled out in the previous chapter? In many parishes the pastoral council is on the margins of parish life. The pastor and some eight to twelve people gather once a month to listen to reports, discuss pressing issues, offer advice to the pastor, and then adjourn. It is not something any of the participants look forward to with much relish. This includes the pastor.

There is an alternative. Bring the pastoral council to the center of the leadership mix. Make it the "glue" for all that happens in the parish. Begin by redefining the role and purpose of the council. The key words are "mission," "model," "focus," "decisions," and "crisis."

1. *Mission:* Section One of this book dealt with what is unique about the parish, which in turn led to the formation of a parish mission statement. This is a major function of the pastoral council, to explore what are the core values and essential elements of the parish. The council, with the pastor as an equal member and active participant, raises up the core values and mission of the parish. This serves as a guide and unifier for the goals and action plans established by the commissions, committees, ministries, and organizations of the parish.

70

2. Model: This is a key function of the pastoral council. To be a member of the council implies that the person has been involved in various ministries and groups within the parish and has served for a year on one of the five commissions described in the previous chapter. As a result of this experience, all those on the pastoral council know what a good meeting should look like, are able to accomplish tasks in a collaborative manner, are willing to share their wisdom and insights with one another, can deal with conflicts as they arise, and know how to pray with others and to enjoy one another's company. The pastoral council, in other words, is the model for other leadership groups to emulate. When the council runs into difficulties, as all groups eventually do, it knows where to turn for help and facilitation, either to a resource within the parish or someone from outside. The pastor and council work together at maintaining this high level of sharing and effectiveness, encouraging other groups to do the same. Every time the council meets it is a productive and enjoyable experience for all concerned.

3. Focus: Another essential task of the council is to provide a common direction or focus for the parish as a whole. This may take the form of a yearly theme, which the various leadership groups and ministries can use in setting goals and making decisions about their future. One multi-cultural parish, for example, chose "Bridging the Cultures" as its theme. This became the constant mantra of the parish for an entire year. It appeared on banners, in the bulletin, on the website, in meeting rooms, on cards in the pews — always in the languages of the various ethnic groups in the parish. All the parishioners knew its meaning and significance, that "we are one parish, not two or three." Other possible themes include "All Are Welcome," "Discovering Our Call," "A Community for Others," "On a Mission," "Believing Is Seeing." The pastoral council might also rally the parish around a central project, such as building a new church, school, or pastoral center, or around a mission project in which the parish adopts a sister parish in the diocese or at some other location. The entire parish, and every ministry, program, or

71

organization in it, is heading in the same direction because of this common theme or focus articulated by the council. The council becomes the glue, the impetus, the initiator, and the instigator at the center of the parish community.

4. *Decisions:* Decision making is another important function of the pastoral council. Not that it makes all the decisions itself, just as the pastor or staff is not the only decider of what happens in the parish. Rather, the council acts as the arbitrator and discerner in trying to determine which group or individual should be the decider regarding a particular project or issue.[10] The role of the council is to "decide who decides." The pastor and council, working as a single, collaborative unit, discern whether a particular decision belongs to the pastor, staff, council, commission, committee, task group, or key individual. This "deciding who decides" arises only if there is confusion and ambiguity about where a decision belongs. As a prayerful, discerning body at the center of parish life, the pastoral council is best equipped to funnel the decision-making process to the appropriate group or individual. Not only does the council place the decision where it belongs but also gives those making the decision the freedom to decide without having to return to the council for approval or ratification.

5. *Crisis:* All parishes face crises, both smaller ones related to a particular ministry or project, and larger ones that affect a number of groups or the parish as a whole. For these larger crises, it is the job of the council to confront them squarely and discern the best course of action to follow. No longer is the pastor left holding the parish together all by himself. The pastoral council works with the pastor in partnership to figure out the best way to proceed or best course to follow. The crisis may be of long duration, such as planning for an expanding or dwindling church population, constructing a new building, or discerning how best to cluster with a neighboring parish. The crisis might happen suddenly, such as a fire or natural disaster, the unexpected death of a staff member or key leader, a sudden shift in personnel or transition in leadership. The

council is positioned as the central body of the parish to handle these crises, always with the pastor as an integral member of this body. The advent of modern technology allows for instant communication and rapid discernment of ideas and opinions when a crisis arises. Some of these crises can be dealt with at regularly scheduled meetings; others may demand a special session or some other form of "deliberation at a distance." Whatever method is used, a key function of the pastoral council is to work in concert with the pastor in dealing with parish-wide crises, if and when they occur.

Council Structures

Pastoral councils have many ways of structuring themselves, many options for choosing their membership, many variations for how they might function. After much experimenting and direct experience, the model presented here, as well as in the previous chapter, has proven effective in many parishes. It begins with how people are chosen to be members of the pastoral council.

If the council is to be a model group in the parish, it must have members who are experienced in leadership and who are aware of all that is happening in the parish. The best way to achieve this level of expertise and knowledge is to choose members from among those already involved in leadership positions. This is in contrast to picking people from the parish "at large." The latter method is a common one, whether through a parish-wide election, picking people by lot from a list of candidates, or discerning members from a group of nominees called forth for this purpose. The difficulty with this "at large" approach is that once people are on the council it tends to become a separate entity which is independent of other leadership bodies and ministries in the parish. In some parishes, once people get on the council they must choose a leadership group with which to connect, such as a liturgy committee or formation board. The council person acts as the liaison with that body. It often happens, however, that the council person is unaware of how

73

the group operates or what its role and function are. By the time the council liaison person becomes familiar with a committee or ministry the person's term is up and it is time to leave the council.

As an alternative, consider the commission structure described in chapter 8. In the example used there you were a member of the Sunday morning choir and eventually were chosen as one of the founding members of a new worship commission. The commitment was for six months, but at the end of that time, having enjoyed the interaction with the rest of the group and the sense of accomplishment, you decide to continue on the commission for a full three-year term. Being a co-chair was a good experience but you felt it was time to give that position over to someone else. For the first six months of experimentation, two members from the existing pastoral council had joined the worship commission as a way of fostering a closer connection between the council and commissions. This was only an interim and temporary arrangement. When one of the two council members' term was up, this left an opening for someone from the worship commission to become a member of the pastoral council. Through a discernment process involving all of the commission members, you were chosen to fill that vacancy. For the next two years you served concurrently on both the commission and the pastoral council. The beauty of this arrangement was that it did not demand an extra meeting night. At the conclusion of the commission's one-hour meeting and the two-minute reports, the pastoral council, after a short time for refreshments and socializing, met for the final forty-five minutes of the evening. With the Leadership Night starting at 7:00 p.m., you were still able to be on your way home shortly after 9:30 p.m.

As this new structure came into being and the terms of existing pastoral council members were completed, new members were discerned from each of the five commissions to fill those positions. Eventually, two people from each commission made up the pastoral council, together with the pastor and the pastor's co-leader, the parish administrator. This brought the total membership to twelve people. The term of office on the council was two years, one person coming off of the council and another joining it each year. Most of the orientation for the council members had already taken place when they joined one of the commissions. You soon discovered that operating as a pastoral council member was a natural progression from being part of a commission. As the new structure took hold, continuity was assured as people first served on the commission and then on both the council and commission for the last two years of their tenure.

The process of choosing co-chairs for the council each year is similar to choosing co-chairs for the commission. In order to spread out the roles and duties of those on the commission, no one who is a member of the pastoral council should also be a co-chair of the commission. If a co-chair is selected to be a member of the pastoral council, someone else will need to be chosen as the new co-chair of the commission. On the pastoral council, however, any two of the ten representatives from the commissions are eligible for being a co-chair of the council. New co-chairs are chosen at the beginning of each year's term, although one person who had been a co-chair the previous year could remain as the "veteran" and a new person selected to be the person's partner in leading the meetings. The selection of co-chairs all depends on a good balance of talents and abilities between the two chosen.

Communication Structures

How will the parishioners as a whole discover what the commissions and council do each month? If interested, they could come and sit in on the Leadership Night. Few, if any, however, have the time or interest to do so. Even posting the minutes of the meeting on a bulletin board reaches only a small percentage of parishioners.

A better method is to have one of the two pastoral council members from each commission write up a short summary at the end of the one-hour meeting about what was accomplished. This would be a written version of the two-minute verbal report given to the whole body at the conclusion of the commission meetings. The written summary is taken to the pastoral council, which meets at the end of the evening. A summary of what the council was about, along with the five summaries from the commissions, is typed up and made available to the parishioners as an insert in the bulletin each month, as well as posted on the parish website. Another regular task for council members from each commission is to send an email soon after the council meeting to all those on the commission. This is a way of filling them in about what transpired at the council meeting. Otherwise it would be a whole month until the next Leadership Night before commission members found out what happened at the council meeting, what decisions were made, and what issues were handled by the council at the conclusion of the Leadership Night.

Questions

1. How does the current pastoral council operate, and how is it connected to other leadership groups in the parish?

2. What would have to change to bring the pastoral council to the center of parish life and allow it to be the "glue" that holds everything else together?

Chapter Ten

Inviting People to Leadership

Finding qualified people to serve on the commissions is a major requirement for a productive leadership structure. The type of person best suited for this job is someone willing to put the mission of the parish into practice. To do this, the person needs to be able to look beyond what *is* and envision what *could be* in one of the five areas of worship, community life, formation, outreach, and administration. This entails observing carefully what is happening in the parish, interacting and linking with parish groups and individuals related to the commission, and writing engaging and creative goals as a way of taking this one area of the parish to the next level of growth and spiritual development.

A commission member must also be willing to work in partnership with others and not be afraid to speak up and share concerns or insights whenever necessary or appropriate. The person must also have the best interests of the one key area covered by the commission in mind and not promote the issues or agenda of a particular ministry or pet project.

On the practical side, all members of the commission must be willing to attend the monthly Leadership Night and link up with one or more groups or ministries associated with the commission each and every month. Young adults should be encouraged to participate as members of the commission, but they must be at least sixteen years of age and be active, registered members of the parish.

Getting on a Commission

At the beginning, when this new structure is first being formed, individuals are invited to an orientation meeting and are then asked to be part of an interim commission structure for a six-month interval in order to get it off the ground. At the end of this experimental period, those who are willing remain on the commission as the first members of the new "official" commission. If not all nine people are willing to serve, new people are chosen to fill the vacancies but only after being given an orientation using the Covenant Booklet or leadership manual as a guide.

One of the first tasks of the official commission will be to discern who among the nine members will serve a one-, two-, or three-year term. This sets up a staggered tenure of membership so that each year one-third of the group is replaced by new recruits. This process for adding new members to the commission each year, called the Yearly Gathering of Ministers, is best done during Lent. It has three stages: *nominations, gathering, selection.*

1. *Nominations:* The first step is to ask parishioners to nominate those whom they feel would make good commission members. The qualities for this position are listed in the bulletin, included on the website, and mentioned during the announcements at Mass. Those active in ministries and groups are also invited and encouraged to nominate someone for the commission. This is done for a number of weeks leading up to the "Nomination Weekend." Current commission members give a brief "witness talk" at all of the weekend liturgies, explaining the commission structure, what takes place on the Leadership Night, the qualities and expectations for new members, and what being on the commission has meant to them. They

then invite people to fill out a nomination form located in the pews. A form might look something like this:

Invitation

Do you know someone who would make a good member of a commission, someone good at leadership, at looking ahead and visioning, at making decisions, at interacting and connecting with parish groups and organizations? Write down that person's name, and he or she will be invited to attend an "Invitation to Leadership" night a week from next Wednesday.

Nominee's Name _____

Address _____

Phone _____

Special gifts you see in this person:

_____

_____

Ministries or groups in which the person is now active:

_____

_____

Your own name: _____

The same nomination form is handed out at all parish gatherings during the weeks leading up to the Nomination Weekend. It is also included as an insert in the bulletin, placed on a table in the gathering area outside of church, and kept in all parish offices and meeting rooms. Those on the commissions also nominate people whom they feel would make good candidates, personally inviting them to attend the Invitation to Leadership night.

2. *Gathering of Ministers:* All the nomination sheets are collected, collated, and sent to a special ad hoc committee which then makes phone calls and sends letters to all those named as candidates, making a personal invitation to them to come to the special Gathering

of Ministers. Announcements at the Masses and in the bulletin make clear that everyone is invited and encouraged to attend, whether nominated or not. The announcement mentions that this would be a good occasion for finding out more about the parish and how the commission structure operates.

The Gathering of Ministers itself usually takes two hours, beginning with prayer and ending with a social. After the prayer there is an overview of the evening and an explanation of the leadership structure. Then the assembly divides into five areas of ministry. All those attending are asked to choose one of the five possible areas: worship, community life, formation, outreach, or administration. Everyone is given a structure diagram similar to the example on the facing page to help them determine which area to attend. Ordinarily those active in one of the ministries or groups associated with an area will choose that one to attend, but they are not required to do so.

The co-chairs for each commission lead the discussion for their area, explaining what the commission has accomplished over the last year and what goals it is working on for the coming year. All of the current members, as well as the staff resource person, are introduced and have a chance to offer their insights and observations. All present are encouraged to ask questions or give feedback.

Then the nomination process begins. Those who had been nominated are identified and asked if they would be willing to serve if chosen to do so. One of the commission members makes clear that being nominated does not automatically mean the person will be on the commission. Rather, the names of all who are willing to serve are brought to the next Leadership Night. It is at that meeting, using a discernment process, that the commission will choose the three new members, making sure there is a good cross-section of ages, backgrounds, and experience in the parish. Those willing to keep their names on the nomination list are asked to fill out a consent sheet that includes the person's name, phone, email addresses, and the name of the commission that the person is willing

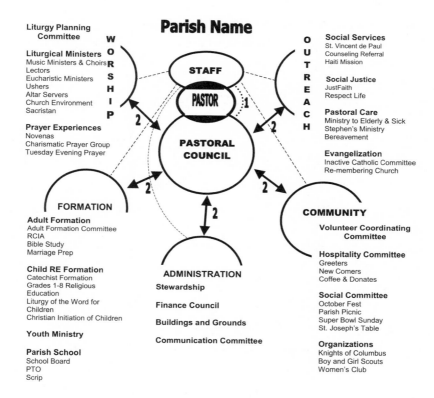

Parish Name

Liturgy Planning Committee

Liturgical Ministers
Music Ministers & Choirs
Lectors
Eucharistic Ministers
Ushers
Altar Servers
Church Environment
Sacristan

Prayer Experiences
Novenas
Charismatic Prayer Group
Tuesday Evening Prayer

WORSHIP

STAFF

PASTOR

PASTORAL COUNCIL

OUTREACH

Social Services
St. Vincent de Paul
Counseling Referral
Haiti Mission

Social Justice
JustFaith
Respect Life

Pastoral Care
Ministry to Elderly & Sick
Stephen's Ministry
Bereavement

Evangelization
Inactive Catholic Committee
Re-membering Church

FORMATION

Adult Formation
Adult Formation Committee
RCIA
Bible Study
Marriage Prep

Child RE Formation
Catechist Formation
Grades 1-8 Religious Education
Liturgy of the Word for Children
Christian Initiation of Children

Youth Ministry

Parish School
School Board
PTO
Scrip

ADMINISTRATION

Stewardship

Finance Council

Buildings and Grounds

Communication Committee

COMMUNITY

Volunteer Coordinating Committee

Hospitality Committee
Greeters
New Comers
Coffee & Donates

Social Committee
October Fest
Parish Picnic
Super Bowl Sunday
St. Joseph's Table

Organizations
Knights of Columbus
Boy and Girl Scouts
Women's Club

to join. Those eventually selected to become members would attend their first Leadership Night two months after this Gathering of Ministers, as well as an orientation session conducted by those leaving the commission. The names of people nominated but not chosen are kept in case there is a vacancy sometime throughout the year.

After the nomination and consent process is completed, all five subgroups return to the large gathering where all who are willing to serve come forward so that those present can pray over them, give them a blessing, and congratulate them for their willingness to serve on a commission. Refreshments and socializing round out the Invitation to Leadership, Gathering of Ministers evening.

3. *Selection:* The primary task for the next Leadership Night is for each commission to decide on the new members of the next three-year term. After the common prayer, each commission gathers for the discernment process. It begins by reading out loud the qualities and expectations for commission members as a way of making sure qualified persons are chosen. People, in other words, are not selected just to fill an open slot but because they best represent a balanced cross-section of men and women, ages, backgrounds, and length of parish membership. The co-chairs explain that it would be better to have fewer people on the commission than to include someone not equipped to carry out the role and responsibilities of the commission. Better, too, to have married couples serve on different commissions rather than being on the same one, at least as a general policy.

Next comes a reflection on the list of nominees. Everyone considers privately each person on the list and reflects on any talents or experiences the person might have to offer or any drawbacks to being chosen. Commission members then share with one another both positive aspects and any reservations they might have for each candidate. After listening to one another, each individual writes on an index card, in order of priority, the names of the three persons best suited to join the commission. These names are listed for all to see. Five points are assigned to one's first choice, three points to the second choice, and one point to the third choice. The numbers are added up, and the three candidates with the most points are selected as the new members. Those going off of the commission are paired up with the new candidates so they can contact them and give them an orientation session using the covenant booklet as a guide. The co-chairs also make sure that a phone call is made and a letter sent to all those not selected, explaining the need to get a cross-section of people on the commission and encouraging these people to remain active in parish ministries and groups so they might be considered as likely candidates to a commission in the future. They are also told that they might be called on to join a commission if and when there is an opening during the coming year.

At the conclusion of the hour, all the commissions come together to give a report on the ones chosen as the new members. These are the people who will join the commissions at the next Leadership Night, along with those going off the commissions as a way of handing over this ministry of leadership, visioning, and oversight to the "new guard." A list of requirements for membership follows:

Qualities and Expectations of a Commission Member

1. Be willing to represent the parish mission statement in visioning and goal setting

2. Be a good observer of what is happening in the parish, and be able to interact well with parishioners

3. Be able to plan and vision, while leaving the implementation to others

4. Come prepared for the commission meetings and prayerfully reflect on what will be discussed and deliberated

5. Stay in touch with other members of the commission in order to remain informed between meetings

6. Be willing to speak up and share your wisdom whenever necessary and appropriate, both in commission meetings and in other parish groups and gatherings

7. Be willing to connect (link) regularly with one or more groups or ministries associated with the commission

8. Be actively involved in a ministry or group associated with the commission

9. Attend the monthly Leadership Night with no more than two absences per year throughout the three-year term

10. Have an active prayer life and be a regular attendee at the liturgies and key functions of the parish

11. Be sixteen years of age or older and a registered member of the parish[11]

Commissioning

The final part of "Inviting People to Leadership" is to ratify the selection of new candidates before the parish community. This is done either in May at the end of the academic year or in September at the start of a new one. Of these two options, September works best because not only are new commission persons in place by that time but so are new pastoral council members. At one of the Leadership Nights during the summer, each commission selects the individual who will be the replacement on the pastoral council for the person completing a two-year term. Typically this is one of the commission members who has been on the commission for a year and has learned how the system works and how the structure operates.

During the early part of September, all the commission and council members attending a particular weekend Mass are called forward to receive a blessing from the congregation as a way of helping the leaders in their deliberations, visioning, and decision making throughout the coming year. At the same time, the new members are given special "Leadership Name Tags" to wear at all parish functions during the year. The pictures of all council and commission members are displayed in the vestibule or gathering area of the church, as well as published in the bulletin and on the website. In this way, parishioners will recognize them and will have a chance to connect with them if they have a concern or question about any aspect of parish life and operation.

Questions

1. What process is now being used to recruit people for leadership positions?

2. What changes would have to take place to initiate a process similar to that described in this chapter?

Section Three

Planning for a Hopeful Future

I will give you shepherds after my own heart,
who will feed you with knowledge and understanding.

—Jeremiah 3:15

The parish now has a clear sense of mission and purpose, as well as a structure by which to carry out this mission. The skeleton of the body is in place, but there is no flesh or muscle on it. This comes with visioning, which flows from the mission statement and provides a desired outcome for each and every aspect of parish life and ministry. Vision is the broad sweep for each of the five aspects of parish life and operation. This broad sweep is made specific through a series of goals that take the parish in a new direction and foster active involvement by the parishioners. It is the role of the commissions to clarify the vision and establish goals in each of the five specific areas. The mission remains the same; the vision and goals adapt to fit changing situations and circumstances.

Chapter Eleven

To Get the Real Scoop — Ask the Folks

The first step in a good planning process is gathering information. What's happening? How do people feel? What do they like or don't like; what gets them excited or frustrated? What, in other words, is the "real scoop"? One definition of apathy is "someone working on someone else's goals." "Who cares?" people say. "No one asked our opinion. And what difference will it make anyway? Why bother?" If interest and involvement by parishioners is a desired outcome, then they need to be asked their opinions *before* any plans are made. The difficulty is how to accomplish this in a parish numbering in the hundreds or, more likely, thousands.

Uncovering Attitudes

The Parish Evaluation Project (PEP) was founded in the early 1970s as a way of uncovering what parishioners were thinking and feeling. As part of a dissertation, I interviewed all the priests in a cross-section of parishes covering a wide range of educational, ethnic, and economic backgrounds. I began by asking the priests about the attitudes and desires of the parishioners. I then surveyed the people themselves. The results were revealing. Comparing what the priests said and how the people responded, I discovered that the clergy knew the thoughts and concerns of the more active people but not a cross-section of parishioners. Many came regularly to church but never voiced an opinion or gave the leadership any feedback — not until they were asked directly. At the invitation of an anonymous survey they went on at length about the parish and the church, offering reactions to many religious, moral, and social issues. When I went back to the priests with this information, each one of them, in one form or another, questioned the results and my methodology. "We know our people," one priest remarked. "You must have made some mistake in your analysis."

That comment, along with others, convinced me of the need to provide to the pastor, staff, and lay leaders accurate information about parishioners' attitudes and feelings concerning the parish. Only then could they make good plans for the future. Now, almost forty years later, the mandate remains: "ask the folks" before making any major plans or important decisions. Many of those in parish leadership still rely on their own hunches, guesses, and intuitions for setting new directions in the parish. Such an approach is a breeding ground for apathy, frustration, anger, and withdrawal.

There are many ways to uncover attitudes. These range from personal observation and attentive listening to well-organized, formal methods of information gathering. Such a simple approach as sending out all the commission members to pay attention, ask questions, and gather data between one Leadership Night to the next will uncover a wealth of information and insights about the parish. On the formal side, there are many options, three of which are described below: surveying, town hall meetings, and personal interviews.

Surveying

"Let's take a survey" is a frequent suggestion at commission meetings. Once into the effort, it can bog down a group for months with little to show for it. Rule of thumb: keep any survey short, simple, and focused, and don't try to ask everyone's opinion. Take, for instance, the effort to get feedback about the weekend liturgies. A half-sheet survey containing six or seven questions is sufficient.[12] Hand it out randomly to twenty-five people as they come into Mass. Ask the recipients to fill it out at the end of Mass and give it to one of the ushers or drop it in the "survey box" at the back of church. Print the half sheet on stiff paper and supply people with a pen or pencil to make it easy for them. Pass out the surveys at one Mass each weekend over a number of weeks. Such a simple exercise will reap a wealth of information about the liturgies that can shape future plans and directions. If this were done before and soon after the introduction of greeters to the Masses, as mentioned in chapter 8, the planners might discover which liturgies were most open to this ministry and what adaptations or "tweaking" might be necessary.

It also helps to do a "before" and "after" assessment when anything new is introduced, whether related to the liturgies or anything else in the parish. A short survey distributed at random to a small group of people will uncover how they feel about any change, addition, or deletion. A follow-up survey will show whether anyone noticed the difference and whether they liked it or not.

As part of the Parish Assessment and Renewal (PAR) process, we survey a cross-section of parishioners as the first step in the information gathering phase. The parish leadership, with our help and direction, makes up a survey instrument. Even in a large parish with a few thousand or more members, a random sample of three to four hundred individual adults — not family units — is sufficient. This sample is constructed from a set of random numbers that is matched to the parish census file. Anyone can make up a list of random numbers. Knowing the total number of adult parishioners, say 3,000, choose 300 random numbers from the 3,000. The list might begin with the numbers 5, 9, 21, 25, 37, 42, etc. Go through the census file and pick out the 5th adult 18 years of age or older, then the 9th, the 21st, and so forth. The result will be a group of

300 parishioners who reflect the total membership because it was selected by chance. Anyone else who might want to fill out a survey could do so, but the random sample surveys are kept separate as reflective of a cross-section of the parishioners.

The next step is to make up a survey instrument that has five sections based on the five commission areas. The results of each section can be given to commissions to help them make plans and set goals for the future. It might help to have an outside group or organization process the survey results so that anonymity is protected, but this is not necessary. Once given a chance to voice their opinions, parishioners, active as well as inactive, will respond.

In parishes whose members belong to various ethnic groups, more effort may be needed to get a response from these groups, whether Hispanic, Asian, or those of some other heritage. Besides a written survey, the information gathering could also be done over the phone as an interview or a one-on-one sharing after the liturgies or some other parish gathering. Important information can be obtained if surveys are conducted in people's own language and with sensitivity to their schedules and cultural inclinations.

In making up the survey, keep it to five or six pages at the most and no more than fifty questions total. Provide multiple-choice questions, as well as open-ended, "fill in the blank" ones. End the survey with one catch-all question that asks, "Are there any other comments you would like to make about the parish as a whole, or about any of the liturgies, programs, or ministries in particular?" When given the opportunity, people will share their ideas and reactions, sometimes going on at great length.

Once the returns are in, let the parishioners know what will happen with the responses, that what was learned will not be put on a shelf to gather dust. Rather, it will be used by the commissions within the next few months to make plans for the future. People are also told where they can obtain a summary of the findings.[13]

Town Hall Meetings

Another way to "ask the folks" is to host a gathering of the entire parish. A good time for this is on a Sunday afternoon following the last morning Mass. The gathering need not last more than an hour, and no refreshments before or after are necessary. It is a time where the parishioners can express their opinions in an orderly way and within a short space of time. Begin preparing for the event by stirring up interest with every means possible. Let people know that their ideas and suggestions will lead to changes in the parish; they will have a chance to contribute to important plans and new directions.

As for the event itself, set up the space so there is a place for everyone to gather in one area for the opening prayer and personal reflection. Plan for one to two hundred participants. Arrange the rest of the space for small groups of seven or eight people each. This can be done around tables or simply with a circle of chairs. Ask commission members to be the reporters for each of the small groups. Prepare for about twenty to twenty-five groups in all.

As people arrive have them make a name tag for themselves and give them an index card that has a number on it from one to twenty-five. This will indicate which small group they will be in after the opening prayer. If there is ethnic diversity in the parish, those whose first language is Spanish, Vietnamese, or some other are given index cards with numbers matching their language group.

Following a brief welcoming statement by the pastor or pastoral council member and an opening prayer, each person is asked to write on the index card responses to these three questions:

1. What are three things we should *keep* doing as a parish? We can't let go of these; they are very important.

2. What are three things we should *stop* doing? We don't need them anymore; they are not helpful to us as a parish.

3. What are three things we should *start* doing? These are new things or ways of operating that would make this a better parish.

People are invited to use some quiet time for reflection, writing their responses to the three questions on their index card. Toward the end of this exercise those assigned to be the recorders are sent off to their tables or circle of chairs while everyone else remains where they are. The recorders hold up high the number of their group for all to see. Once the recorders are in place, everyone is told to find the group that matches the number listed on their index card.

In the small groups, the recorders begin by asking people to introduce themselves, writing their names on the back of the re-port sheet for future reference. Then, starting with one person, the recorder asks for one idea of something the parish should *keep* doing, writing the person's response on the report sheet. Then the next person gives an idea, and so forth around the circle of people. The recorder also adds ideas as a member of the group. If any items are repeated, they are not listed twice, only acknowledged, and then the recorder asks for another idea from the person, which is then added to the report sheet.

The recorder goes around the group three times to gather all of the suggestions people have about what the parish should keep doing. This same procedure is used for recording the responses to what to *stop* doing, and what to *start* doing. This listing of ideas will take approximately thirty minutes. The recorders are instructed beforehand to keep discussion to a minimum until all of the ideas have been listed. Only then, if time permits, do they encourage people to discuss what was said in the group. It helps to have one or two facilitators walking around the room to keep all the small groups on track, making sure that one or another group is not getting bogged down in discussing a particular issue until the responses to all three questions are recorded.

Toward the end of the small group session each recorder, with the help of the others in the group, picks out one idea from one of the three questions to bring back to the full assembly as an example of what was shared. The recorders from the first third of the small groups bring back one idea of what to *keep* doing, the middle third one idea of what to *stop* doing and the last third one idea of what to *start* doing. The sharing of one result from each of the groups provides a sampling of what was discussed and some awareness of how people reacted to the questions.

The report sheets from all of the small groups are collected, typed up, and given to the commissions to help direct their goal setting and future planning. A summary of what was learned is made available to the parishioners, either through a special mailing, a parish newsletter, an insert into the bulletin, or a listing on the website.

Personal Interviews

A third method for gathering information is one-on-one interviews. This is a valuable tool for getting underneath the surface and discovering "the real scoop." No more than thirty or forty interviews need to be conducted, but each one should have a common format and the same questions in order to process and analyze the results.

Suppose a pastor wants to know what are some of the pressing issues and concerns in the parish. He might enlist the help of a few interviewers from among the parishioners, people who are good listeners and can instill trust and confidence in others. Two or three interviewers might invite the staff, council, commission members, or heads of groups and ministries to answer a few questions about the parish. Three examples of interview questions might be:

1. If everything went right and money was not an object, what would you like to see happen in the parish over the next five years? What, in other words, would you like to see in place by that time?

2. What might get in the way of this desired outcome or future? What, in other words, are the blocks, obstacles, or hindrances that would hold us back?

3. What are a few concrete steps we could take right now, within the next twelve months, that would help us overcome the blocks and move us closer to a better future? What could we do right now to get started?

Each interview would take about forty-five minutes to an hour and could be scheduled over the space of a week to ten days. Those interviewed would be told by the interviewer that no comments would be identified as coming from a particular person, but a summary report of the findings would be shared with the pastor and leadership.

Once completed, the results from each question would be typed up and given to the pastor, staff, council, and commissions to help them in constructing goals and action steps. The interviewers might also sit down with key decision makers or meet with various commissions and provide them with impressions and "feeling tones" that would help explain the significance of the results. This is one advantage of face-to-face interviewing; it provides nuances and insights that cannot be obtained through other methods.

Trust is the key factor. If people know their confidences will be maintained and their responses treated with respect and not used against them, they will reveal a great deal about what they feel needs to be known and heard by the parish leadership.

Both the interview method of gathering information and the town hall process can be used to great advantage when a significant shift in leadership is about to take place, such as a change of pastors, or when the construction of a new building is being planned, or some significant decision faces the parish. This could be the first step in a much larger discernment process involving the entire parish.[14]

Assessing the Liturgy

What follows (on page 98) is a short survey of attitudes that can be printed on a half sheet of card stock and handed out at random to twenty-five people as they enter church. They fill it out before they leave Mass, giving it to one of the ushers or putting it in "survey return" boxes at the doors. The results are tabulated and given to those planning the liturgies and those in charge of the various liturgical ministries. This assessment could be done once a quarter or following a specific liturgical season.

Questions

1. What means are now being used to get in touch with the attitudes and desires of the parishioners?

2. Are the opinions and desires of the less active members and those on the fringes of the parish known and respected?

Evaluation of Liturgy

Please give us your ideas and feedback about this Mass. Thank you for your help.

The Worship Commission

1. Which Mass are you assessing? Check one.

o 4:00 PM Saturday	o 7:30 AM Sunday	o 10:30 AM Sunday
o 5:30 PM Saturday	o 9:00 AM Sunday	o 12:00 AM Sunday

2. In general, what is your attitude toward this Mass?

o Very favorable	o Favorable	o Mixed feelings	o Unfavorable

Why? _____
_____

3. What is your attitude toward the sense of welcoming?

o Very favorable	o Favorable	o Mixed feelings	o Unfavorable

Why? _____
_____

4. What is your attitude toward the music used at this Mass?

o Very favorable	o Favorable	o Mixed feelings	o Unfavorable

Why? _____
_____

5. What is your attitude toward the homily?

o Very favorable	o Favorable	o Mixed feelings	o Unfavorable

Why? _____
_____

6. Does the environment of the church help you pray?

o Yes, definitely	o Somewhat	o Probably not	o Not at all

Why? _____
_____

7. In what ways could this Mass be improved?

_____
_____
_____

Chapter Twelve

Focusing the Information
Settling on Specifics

Translating information into plans for the future is no easy task. It demands a clear focus of what was uncovered and an intuition of what was important in the findings. Suppose the parish leadership took to heart the mandate to "ask the folks." They surveyed people's opinions, held parish-wide town hall meetings, and interviewed a number of individuals to discover what people thought about the life and operation of the parish — what was going well and what more was needed. The information was collected, but now what? Where to go from here?

Focusing the Information

The first task is to translate the information into a usable format. For a survey, this means not only recording the results from each question but highlighting significant findings, making comparisons between subgroups, such as leaders vs. parishioners, men vs. women, young vs. old. People also write comments to explain their answers. These opinions need to be typed up and categorized so that patterns and trends emerge when a number of comments coalesce around a similar reaction or a number of comments follow the same line of thought. The task is to look *through* the data in order to discover what people are trying to say. For instance, parishioners may complain about baptisms during Mass. Looking more closely at the information reveals that the ritual is too drawn out and, as people view it, just another thing added to the Mass that is already too long. Instead of people leaving with a positive attitude, they go out angry and frustrated. This is not the time to solve the problem. That comes later. What is needed now is to discover from the survey results as much as possible about what people found distasteful. The baptism itself may have been meaningful but not all the "extras" added on. Was it really necessary to sing all the verses to the songs? Could the homily be shorter or could there be fewer announcements when there is a baptism? All this information is available for those who look closely at the results and try to make sense out of what was being said.

The same effort at collecting and focusing information is also necessary when analyzing the results from a town hall meeting. Each small group of seven to eight people produced a report of how individuals responded to the questions of what to *keep* doing, *stop* doing, or *start* doing. These sheets need to be typed up and summarized so that those making plans for the future can see what was frequently mentioned in each of these three categories. For instance, the lively, contemporary music used at the Sunday evening liturgy was affirmed as something to keep doing. "It keeps our young people involved," was one of the comments made. But in the area of "stop doing," others mentioned the need for balance. "Keep the music at the 5:00 p.m. Sunday liturgy," was one response, "but make it more conducive to congregational singing and not a performance by the music group."

Writing up the results from personal interviews requires the same attention to trends and patterns. Not every comment is significant, but when added together there emerges a clarity about what is going well, what is getting in the way, and what more is needed.

A Writers Group

Once the information is summarized and focused so that it can be studied and analyzed, the next step is to assemble a small "writers group" to synthesize the results and write up a report of the findings. It is the task of this group to take all the results and arrange, focus, and highlight them so that others can make plans based on this information. Using the structure suggested in chapter 8, the writers group prepares separate report materials for each of the five commissions of worship, community life, formation, outreach, and administration.

The five to seven people in this writers group are chosen for their ability to make sense out of all the information that lies before them and identify key areas of concern and need. This would include a report of the survey results, together with the written comments that reveal people's feelings and desires. There would also be a compilation of the town hall meeting results, showing what people favored, what they were willing to let go of, and what they would like to see initiated in the parish. Added to these results would be a summary of the personal interviews, indicating what a representative group of leaders and parishioners would like to see the parish become, what gets in the way, and where to begin making changes in order to reach the desired outcome.

The writers group studies the results and then spells out key issues and findings for each of the commissions. Consider a parish in which one common thread related to worship was the length of the Masses. This put a strain on parking and caused frustration for those leaving and coming to church as they got in each other's way. A second concern was music, especially involving the congregation in the singing. A third was providing a more welcoming, hospitable spirit at the Masses. Another issue was the preaching. People asked for concrete ideas and insights that they could bring home with them and that would stay with them throughout the week. A fifth need was the church environment, which included

101

not only decorations but the lighting and sound system as well. A sixth key area was providing prayer experiences outside of the Masses that would speak to the needs of various age groups and different ethnic backgrounds. Taking each of these six headings, the writers group made up a paragraph on each one showing what information was uncovered and what were some of the people's desires, expectations, and suggestions.

In community life, one significant finding was the need to break down the cliques and barriers between groups and individuals so that no one felt excluded. A second area was the need to welcome newcomers, helping them feel at home and encouraging them to become involved. A third issue was the recruitment and management of volunteers. There was no coordinated effort at this, so each ministry and program was in competition over soliciting people to help out in their area. A fourth request voiced by many was the desire for more social activities so parishioners could get to know each other and have fun together. A fifth was the need to reach out to young adults, those in their twenties and thirties. This age group was getting lost and was not well cared for in the parish. In writing up the paragraph for this last area, the writers group noted, "Engaging young adults in all areas of parish life was the third highest priority coming out of the survey results. There is no group or ministry in the parish coordinating activities for this age group, no liturgy that speaks to their needs, not even any budget for funding young adult events and projects. There is little or no emphasis on the unique concerns and issues facing young singles and married couples. The interviews with younger people revealed hardly any encouragement or helps in discovering ways for these people to bond together as a group, enjoy each other's company, or gain insight into how to cope with the pressures of jobs, home life, and personal relationships. The question is how the parish could become a focal point for young adults, offering them a place to share stories and gain insights into what it means to be a Christian in today's fast-paced, consumer-driven, challenging lifestyle."

In formation and faith development, the writers group focused on these five areas: First was the need to integrate the school more into the life of the parish as a whole. Much as the principal, faculty, school board, and parents' organization tried to integrate the school into the life of the parish community, the information uncovered feelings of resentment from those not connected with the school and elitism among some of the parents of schoolchildren. A second issue was better coordination and organization of the religious education program for those attending public schools. Although people liked the director, there was some concern that the catechists were not all doing a good job, nor were they, according to some, adequately trained and supervised. A few people suggested trying out a new approach that would include the parents more, perhaps having joint sessions that would include the parents and children together. Another concern was teenagers. The youth program was well organized, especially the Sunday evening program of Mass, food, and group activities, but it was still reaching only a small fraction of those in this age group. What would entice others to attend? How to include the teen leaders and popular students who, in turn, would encourage others to attend? The area of adult enrichment left much to be desired. There were many individual offerings and opportunities for adult formation throughout the year, but not many people attended and there did not seem to be any overall direction or coordination of these events. People asked for better planning and organization. Some of the participants at the town hall meeting wondered about having a weeklong mission or parish revival, perhaps a series of small group discussions during Lent — anything that would stir up interest and involvement in the area of adult formation and enrichment.

For outreach, a number of issues surfaced that needed attention. Top on the list was connecting with inactive and non-attending parishioners. The survey results showed that less than half of the parishioners attended Mass regularly, but nothing had been done to find out why they were not coming. Because the parish census files had not been updated for a number of years, it was not even clear who these inactive parishioners were and whether they were still members or not. Some concerted effort was needed to learn who were inactive, what their needs might be, and what kept them from attending church. A second issue for outreach was service to the poor and needy. A small group of dedicated people was maintaining the St. Vincent de Paul ministry. Parishioners gave generously when a special need arose, but something more was needed to spark enthusiasm and raise people's awareness of social outreach ministries. Results from the town hall meeting, especially in response to what to *start* doing as a parish, suggested taking on a new service project, such as a poorer parish in the area or a mission in another part of the country or in a foreign land. Greater visibility about what was happening in Christian service was another need uncovered by the information gathering. When asked on the survey whether the parish was doing enough to meet the needs of the poor, many respondents had no opinion. They had no idea what the parish was doing. This led the writers group to highlight that what was needed was greater visibility among parishioners about all that was going on in this area. The report stated that "this emphasis on greater visibility will help all the various social ministries become more present to parishioners and will increase their awareness of each other's activities and ministries as well. It would also make it possible for people to understand what is involved in these outreach ministries and thus make it easier for them to volunteer and become active in these service events and activities." A fourth issue was peace and justice. This was an area mostly untouched by the parish community. Not many homilies centered on justice issues; not many programs or projects had this as their focus. With the exception of the pro-life group, no opportunities existed in the parish to gather parishioners together to discuss such issues as capital punishment, war, torture, global warming, abuse, world hunger, homelessness, or just wages. Despite the reluctance to confront these difficult questions, some of the results from the personal interviews asked whether something could be done to alert parishioners about these critical issues. What seemed to be needed were non-threatening entry points for people to share their thoughts and feelings about injustice and prejudice in a open, non-judgmental, accepting environment. Some of those interviewed also asked that more educational materials and presentations be provided that showed the linkage between Gospel values and social justice issues. The fifth area under outreach concerned pastoral care. The homebound, sick, and elderly were being visited by the priests, the pastoral associate, and a group of volunteers who brought communion to the hospitals and nursing homes. The information gathered revealed, however, the need for a wider definition of pastoral care. Many parishioners were experiencing loss in one form or another. Not only was it the death of a loved one, but loss of job, health, mobility, and income as well. "All those experiencing loss and challenging transitions," the report read, "could benefit from assistance, support, and care from trained volunteers and from the parish community as a whole." The parish was in a unique position to offer this help, but it would need a concerted effort to get such an expanded pastoral care ministry off the ground.

As for administration, five areas surfaced as needing attention. These included finding new ways to communicate with parishioners so that everyone would know what is happening, a better reporting process by the finance council so there are no secrets about where the money comes from and how it is being spent, an update of the parish census that could be easily accessed by staff and leaders, better upkeep of the buildings and grounds in a way that would make people feel proud to belong to the parish, and most of all, a special emphasis on stewardship as a way of life so that people could experience a conversion to give back to God a portion of all they have received.

105

Once completed, the writers group made its report available to the commissions, both in written form and as a verbal presentation at one of the Leadership Nights. It would be up to the commissions to use this focused information as a basis for constructing a strategic plan for the parish that would cover the next three to five years.

Questions

1. What are the ways in which your parish focuses the hopes, desires, and concerns of the parishioners into topics for goal-setting and action planning?

2. What is one thing that needs attention in each of the five areas of worship, community life, formation, outreach, and administration?

Chapter Thirteen

Knowing What Comes Next
Visioning and Writing Goals

A parish without a mission does not know who it is; a parish without a vision does not know where it is going. Chapter 4 described how to clarify the mission and encapsulate it into a short, easy-to-remember statement. Now is the time to form visions that spell out where the parish is heading; what are its hopes and desires for the future?

Consider a gathering of the five commissions on a Saturday morning a few weeks after Easter. Attending this meeting are not only the nine current members of each commission but all those discerned at the last Leadership Meeting as new members of the commissions. This special gathering also includes the entire pastoral staff, not just the five resource persons. The staff splits up so they are well distributed among the various commissions. The purpose of this nine-to-noon meeting is to clarify the vision and set goals for each of the essential aspects of the parish: worship, community life, formation, outreach, and administration.

Vision Statements

The morning begins in a reflective mode as members of each of the five commission groups, now numbering from twelve to fifteen people, consider the broad sweep of what they are trying to accomplish. This is the overriding direction and intent for each aspect of the parish. Participants are given a one-sentence summary of the vision for each of the five areas fashioned by the staff. Commission members are asked to pray over the vision statement for their area individually, meditating on how this shapes and helps focus their work on the commission or staff.

For instance, in worship, the sentence reads, *"The celebration of Eucharist is where people can come together for communal prayer and active involvement in worship."* Everything flows from this broad vision. The parish provides a fitting environment where people can congregate to hear the Word, praise and thank their God, ask for help and forgiveness, participate in ritual and song together, be nourished and strengthened through Eucharist for their life journey, be challenged to love tenderly and act justly. All of this is done with the active and full involvement of all those present in liturgy and communal prayer. Whatever goals are written during the day must manifest and be tested against this overall vision. The goals are meant to bring the vision alive and make it visible in the faith community.

For community life, the broad scope is summed up in this vision statement: *"We help build relationships so that people can get to know one another, have fun together as a community, and share their time, energy, and skills through active involvement in the parish."* Those reflecting on this statement might think of what it would look like if this vision were fully realized. Everyone would feel welcomed and accepted. Many different socials and gatherings would be taking place throughout the year. Parishioners would bond with one another and friendships would flourish. A large cadre of volunteers would be helping out with all facets of parish life and operation.

In the formation and faith development area, the broad vision is this: *"We are committed to lifelong learning and to discovering who God is in our lives."* Staff members and commission people associated with formation might think about inter-generational learning, people of different ages and ethnic backgrounds coming together to learn about their faith. People would be sharing with each other what their faith has meant to them, how God has been revealed in their work, family, and individual experiences. This learning goes on throughout one's life as people discover new insights, images, and challenges with each successive stage of living.

For outreach, the vision statement reads, *"We are sent to care for the sick, to reach out to those in need, to connect with those on the fringes of parish life, and to confront injustice and prejudices in any form."* It might dawn on those meditating on this vision what a large order this is, but to be a Christian requires a reaching out to others. They might also ponder what a witness the parish could become if it were to live up to this image of pastoral care and social justice. This is not a task for a few committed social servants or pastoral caretakers but a ministry for the parish community as a whole. To be a service-oriented parish means living the Christian life to the fullest.

The vision statement for administration states, *"We are being good stewards of our limited resources, providing the physical and financial means so all the other ministries and groups can realize their fullest potential, making sure that all channels of communication between leaders and people are kept open and moving in both directions."* Those involved in this area might reflect on how essential their unique ministry is in the parish, that without the support and maintenance of administration nothing else would happen. The challenge is to remain flexible and open to new ways of operating so others feel supported and encouraged to try out new things without undo restrictions or unnecessary constraints.

After ten to fifteen minutes of personal reflection, the staff and commission members count off and gather into random groups of five to six members each. This gives everyone a chance to share insights from all the vision statements and not just in their own area. At the end of this fifteen-minute small group sharing, everyone reassembles for the next step in the process, that of making the broad visions realizable through a set of well-focused goals.

The Caucus

Spread around the room are five large sheets of paper, each one containing the name of a commission and a list of areas needing attention that was created by the "writers group" described in the previous chapter. The five lists are as follows:

Worship

1. Length of Mass
2. Congregational singing
3. Welcoming spirit
4. Memorable homilies
5. Improve environment
6. Prayer experiences

Community Life

1. Cliques & in-groups
2. Welcoming newcomers
3. Managing volunteers
4. More social events
5. Young adults

Formation

1. School and parish
2. Religious education
3. Teenagers
4. Adult enrichment
5. Mission/revival
6. Small groups

Outreach

1. Inactive parishioners
2. Christian service
3. Visibility
4. Peace and justice
5. Pastoral care

Administration

1. Communication
2. Reporting of finances
3. Census update
4. Upkeep of buildings
5. Stewardship

Everyone is asked to "caucus" around the sheet related to their area. By "caucus" I mean a brief gathering of people for quick decision making. No one sits down because time is limited, usually no more than five to seven minutes. In this case, commission and staff members are to decide which one of the five to six items on their list would be the focus for their first-year goal, which one for their second-year goal, and which one for their third-year goal. By so doing, the group constructs their strategic plan for the next three years. Once the three items are chosen, individuals put their own names next to the topic for which they would be writing a goal. Three or four people volunteer for each topic. This becomes a subgroup responsible for constructing a goal to address one of the three needs chosen by the caucus group. Once these two tasks are completed, all return to the large group.

When people gather around the five topic sheets, they start to realize how difficult it is to come to a decision. They want to address everything all at once and solve the need or problem within the next year or two. They realize, however, that this would not be an effective use of their time. The commissions only meet once a month for an hour at a time. They have to focus their energies if they are going to achieve their goals and come closer to their overall vision.

During the caucus the following choices are made: In worship, the group decides to begin with a goal in which they could experience some success. They choose to focus on "a more welcoming spirit at the liturgies." This would be their first-year emphasis, followed by attending to the length of the Mass for the second year, and improving congregational singing after that. The other three areas on the list could be handled by others, such as the priests and deacons working on meaningful homilies and the administration commission or parish maintenance staff dealing with the lighting and sound system.

In the community life group, the discussion is intense as people share opinions about which topic should come first. The limitation on time helps them come to a consensus. They decide to concentrate on providing more social events and gatherings in the parish. This in turn would help reduce the cliques and in-groups, which was another item on their sheet. For the second year, the emphasis will be on welcoming newcomers. Following that, the commission will tackle the recruitment and management of parish volunteers. Choosing those three leaves the emphasis on young adults untouched. Perhaps, they reason, some of the social events and welcoming efforts could concentrate on these younger adults in particular.

The caucus on formation has a difficult time coming to a consensus until someone mentions the upcoming parish anniversary. "What a good time," the person remarks, "to stage a parish revival or weeklong mission to spark interest and enthusiasm." That becomes the first-year focus, followed by adult enrichment, and then religious education for the third year. This last area will incorporate the school as the emphasis in religious formation shifts to a broader scope that will include all ages together, parents and children alike. Small groups, another topic listed, could be included under adult enrichment.

For outreach, because connecting with inactive parishioners was such a high priority, indicated by the information gathering, the caucus group picks this as the logical place to begin. The second year will be centered on greater visibility in the parish of outreach ministries, and the third-year focus will be on peace and justice, which would be a completely new area for the outreach commission. Christian service and pastoral care already had active groups associated with them; they just needed better coordination and focus.

The administration caucus, in looking over the list of five needs, agrees that knowing the parish membership must be the first priority. As a result, a census update becomes the first-year emphasis, followed by stewardship in the second year and communication for the third. The commission will also work with the finance council in helping it communicate better with the parishioners, as well as with the buildings and grounds committee and maintenance crew regarding upkeep and beautification of the grounds.

People begin to get excited about what could be accomplished once the issues come into focus and are given priority. After the topics are chosen, individuals quickly decide which of the three topics they will concentrate on for writing up a goal. Everyone reassembles for the next step: learning how to write compelling and engaging goal statements.

Writing Goals

A good goal has four ingredients. First, it should describe a desired outcome, a formulation of what "done" looks like. For instance, in worship, a good goal might start out with, "By the year 20__, our liturgies are inclusive, involving celebrations in which everyone plays a part...." The key word is "are," not "will be" or "are becoming," but the liturgies "are" this. It is a fact, a reality, something that is accomplished, a done deal.

A second ingredient is the tone of a goal statement. It should be exciting, challenging, engaging, and even fun for those working on the goal. For people coming onto the commission a year or two later it should be something they can become enthusiastic about and find enticing. We should be able to say, for example, "When people leave our liturgies they are saying to one another, 'Wow! I want to come back to that!'"

Third, a good goal has a built-in measurability so that those working on it know how much is being accomplished along the way and when the goal is completed. For instance, part of a goal associated with the youth of the parish might include a number or percentage that can be measured, such as, "...one-half of all parishioners between the ages of twelve and eighteen are participating in at least one youth event or service project during the year." In the area of worship, a measure of successful liturgies is people arriving on time and not leaving before the final song.

Finally, a good goal can be accomplished through a series of action steps, that move the implementation along step by step toward completion on or before the stated target date. A word of caution: the goal statement itself does not contain the action steps but it is concrete and realizable enough that action steps can be constructed to reach the goal. A sample goal might be: "By the year 20__, the homilies people hear at the weekend liturgies are brief, well-focused, instructive, and applicable to people's lives, leaving them with a few key words or phrases they can remember throughout the week." Although not stated, one of the action steps for achieving this goal could be bringing together those giving the homilies to settle on an ideal length for a homily, as well as discovering memorable words or phrases people could take home and use throughout the week. Other action steps might include soliciting reactions from parishioners about the homilies, having someone time their length or videotape them on occasion, inviting others to join the homily reflection group to provide a wider perspective. The goal, in other words, can be achieved through intermediate, concrete stages.

Once participants of this Saturday morning gathering of staff and commission members learn how to write a goal, then each person is given an index card on which to write a sample goal for either the first-, second-, or third-year goal, depending on the area that each person chose from the list of topics. One-third of each of the five caucus groups writes a first-year goal, another third a second-year goal, and the rest write a third-year goal. Individuals do this goal writing on their own at their places. Then once they are finished they meet with the others who are writing goals on the same topic. Each person reads his or her own goal aloud and listens to everyone else's. As a group, they pick out key phrases they like from each goal and eventually come to a consensus about the combined goal that pleases them the most.

Once completed, they meet with the other two goal-writing groups from the same commission to hear each other's goals, make any changes or refinements necessary for greater clarity and meaning, and then list all three goals on large sheets of paper to be presented to the entire gathering. What follows is the result of their goal-writing exercise.

Goals for the Next Three Years

Worship

First-Year Goal (Welcoming Spirit): By the year 20___, everyone entering church for the weekend liturgies is made to feel welcome, parishioners and strangers alike, and all are encouraged to reach out in a spirit of hospitality to others, both during and after the Mass.

Second-Year Goal (Length of Mass): By the year 20___, although ordinarily lasting no more than an hour, each weekend liturgy is an involving and meaningful celebration of Word, ritual, and sacrament that is unique to the tone and character of those attending each of the weekend Masses.

Third-Year Goal (Congregational Singing): By the year 20___, our liturgies are inclusive celebrations in which both men and women, young and old and those of various ethnic backgrounds, are actively involved in singing and praising God in joyful song.

Community Life

First-Year Goal (Social Events): By the year 20___, there are a number of occasions for people of all ages and backgrounds to come together as a parish community and enjoy one another's company.

Second-Year Goal (Welcoming Newcomers): By the year 20___, all individuals and families new to the parish are personally welcomed into the community, are encouraged to make it their religious home, and are invited to contribute to its life and spirit.

Third-Year Goal (Volunteer Management): By the year 20___, nine hundred members of our parish are involved in at least one ministry, activity, or project, and thus have a sense of pride in contributing to the well-being of the parish community.

Formation

First-Year Goal (Mission/Revival): By the year 20___, the parish has experienced a revival or mission experience in which at least three hundred people have gained a new spiritual awareness and commitment to their faith.

Second-Year Goal (Adult Enrichment): By the year 20___, there are four hundred adult parishioners from both the English-speaking and Spanish-speaking populations who have a better understanding of scripture and a new awareness of their Catholic faith so they are confident in passing it on to their children and to others.

Third-Year Goal (Religious Education): By the year 20___, there are numerous intergenerational religious formation gatherings that reach at least eight hundred people annually and that foster faith development, prayer, fellowship, and celebration in a communal setting.

Outreach

First-Year Goal (Inactive Parishioners): By the year 20___, our parish is connecting with two hundred inactive parishioners, listening to their concerns, and giving them a sense of worth and well-being.

Second-Year Goal (Visibility): By the year 20___, two-thirds of the parishioners are fully aware of all outreach ministries associated with pastoral care, social service, peace and justice, and connecting with inactive parishioners, and at least a third are taking an active part in these ministries.

Third-Year Goal (Peace and Justice): By the year 20___, the parish is providing regular forums for discussing peace and justice issues and is taking active and visible stands on social moral issues based upon Gospel values and church teachings.

Administration

First-Year Goal (Census Update): By the year 20__, the parish has an accurate listing of its active and inactive members that is updated on a yearly basis and can be easily accessed for use by staff, leaders, ministers, and parish organizations.

Second-Year Goal (Stewardship): By the year 20__, every member of the parish community, both young and old, is strongly encouraged to make stewardship a way of life so that they are giving a portion of their time in prayer, their talents in service, and their treasure in financial contributions back to God.

Third-Year Goal (Communications): By the year 20__, all parishioners are kept informed about what is happening in the parish through a wide variety of communication vehicles and are given the opportunity to share their opinions and desires with those in leadership positions.

Questions

1. What is the broad sweep or vision for the area of the parish in which you are most active, or if there is none, what would you like it to be?

2. How are goals determined in your parish and who forms them, or if none are formed, who should be doing this?

Chapter Fourteen

Translating Goals into Action
Putting Shape to the Plan

The staff and commission members conclude their Saturday morning gathering on a high note. They have accomplished what they set out to do. They now have a clear idea of the vision they want to realize in each of the five commission areas, along with well-focused goals that will carry them over the next three years.

The goal-setting session ends with a ceremony of closure and initiation. This will be the last meeting for those going off the commissions and the first one for those beginning their three-year term. The new goals are hung up in front of all to see. Those whose tenure is completed wish the rest success in achieving the goals. Those remaining ask the staff and "veterans" for prayers to aid them in their efforts. Pastoral council members take upon themselves the task of informing the parishioners about what has happened during the three-hour session, while staff members pledge to talk up the new goals in their own groups and ministries. The goals will also be published in the bulletin, posted on the website, and displayed on large posters around the gathering space leading into church.

The next step is putting the goals into operation. This will happen at the next Leadership Night. All other items will be cleared from the commissions' agenda so this implementation can take place.

Taking Action

The focus of the Leadership Night is the first-year goal for each of the five commissions. For worship, this is fostering a more welcoming spirit at the liturgies. For community life it is creating more parish socials; for formation, a parish mission or revival experience; for outreach, connecting with inactive parishioners, and for administration, updating the census.

As people leave the Saturday morning meeting, each commission member is given a worksheet to work on over the next few weeks. The members are to reflect on the first-year goal for their commission and think of all the ways of reaching the goal, all the action steps that would help the parish move closer to the desired outcome. The worksheet looks like this:

Forming Action Plans

1. Write down a brief description of the first-year goal you will be working on:

   _____

2. Think of all the possible actions that could help reach this goal — any and all ideas, whether practical or just plain crazy.

A. _____   F. _____
B. _____   G. _____
C. _____   H. _____
D. _____   I. _____
E. _____   J. _____

At the next Leadership Night, following the prayer and announcements, the group separates into commissions as is the custom. Led by the staff resource person who acts as the facilitator, the action planning process begins with each person choosing the three *best* ideas from the list of ideas thought up since the goal-setting session. Once people settle on their three best ideas, then they are asked to decide which of the three would be the best one to start with, that is, the action that could take place over the next few months and move the group closer to achieving its first-year goal.

Each person is then given a second worksheet. This one has a breakdown for each month's Leadership Night, along with space for adding action items to each month. The actions are written in the boxes below for each succeeding month, along with who would be responsible for putting each action into operation, what people would need to be consulted before the action takes place, and what might be the victory once the action is completed. The worksheet for the first five months of action planning looks like this:

Commission _____ Date _____ Goal _____					
Months	Jan.	Feb.	March	April	May
Action Items					
PEOPLE to Consult?					
What Is the VICTORY?					

Using this new worksheet as a guide, the commission members share with each other from their list of action items the one each person thinks would be good to start with. Having listened to everyone's suggestions, the group comes to a consensus about the action for the first month and writes this in the first box as their initial action item to be taken up at next month's Leadership Night. In administration, for instance, which had "updating the census files" as its goal, the group decides that the first action should be making up a simple census form. This form could be placed in the pews for the weekend liturgies over a four-week period as a way of updating the census information for at least those who attend church regularly.

As this first action is being written in the "Action Items" box, someone mentions that it might be better to start by forming a special ad hoc census committee that could handle this task. This suggestion shifts the action planning so that now the new focus becomes the formation of a new committee. This changes the first action to spelling out a job description for this group, along with a timeline for implementation. This is an important insight for the administration commission. The members begin to realize that they are not to be the "doers" so much as the instigators and overseers of the actions, thus leaving the implementation of the tasks to others. This gives the commission members a great sense of relief and a new impetus to complete the Action Planning worksheet. The progression becomes clearer. If updating the census is to be given over to a new committee, then the administration commission will need to spell out its expectations for this group and when its task should be completed. Writing up this role definition is left for the next Leadership Night and is put in the first column of the worksheet as the commission's first action item.

The next action is to locate likely candidates to be part of this new census committee. It is much easier to find people to serve on this committee if the task they will be working on is appealing, well-defined, and has a beginning and an end. The life of the committee also has a short time span — four to five months — and there will be a sense of accomplishment at the end, that of locating all or most of the current members of the parish. Soliciting volunteers and forming the committee will be the focus for the Leadership Night two months hence. With any luck, two co-chairs can be located before that time and invited to the commission meeting so they can learn firsthand what their task will be and receive support and encouragement from commission members.

Once the census committee is formed, one of its first jobs will be to make up a short census form to be placed in the pews over four consecutive weekends. Members of the committee will explain the census update process to all those attending Mass, encouraging people to fill out the form — one per household — and return it to an usher or place it in the boxes at the entrances to the church. At the end of the month, committee members, along with other volunteers, will enter the updated information into the parish computer files, making note of the people listed in the file who had not returned the census form. For the missing people, the names and phone numbers will be printed out and separated into sheets containing fifteen to twenty names per sheet. For a parish of two thousand units, this could amount to some thirty to fifty sheets of names for which there is no updated census information.

With all the members of the five commissions as a resource, along with other recruits as needed, each person is asked to take one sheet of names and keep calling people until they get a live person on the line, not an answering machine. This personal contact will do much more than update the census information. It will also show that the parish is interested in the individual enough to make a personal contact. As well as verifying names, addresses, telephone numbers, and email addresses, the callers might also ask whether people have any suggestions or questions about the parish. When appropriate, they could also invite people to take an active part in the parish if they are not already doing so. The names of those who show interest can be funneled to a staff member or ministry head for a follow-up contact.

The census committee will keep track of the calling, requesting that all telephoning be completed within a month's time. What began as a two-thousand-unit parish might end up being only two-thirds that large once the census files are updated.

The administration commission, once it has defined the role of the new census committee and has located people to serve on it, then sets up a timeline for the implementation of the process. Commission members predict that it will take six months from the time the committee is formed until the last census information is added to the parish files. When that happens, both commission and census committee members will come together to celebrate the outcome. At that time not only will the parish membership list be accurate and up-to-date, but there will hopefully be a new computer software program that will provide easy access to the census information by staff and parish leaders. This added action item of locating and installing the new software is a task one of the commission members volunteered to oversee so that once the new census data is ready for entry into the computer files, a new computer program will be in place to receive this information.

Also, as a side effect of the census updating process, the administration commission members hope that the phone calling to those who had not returned a completed census form will provide a wealth of information about what parishioners like, what concerns they have, and who might be willing to take a more active part in parish activities and programs.

This example is only one of many ways in which a goal can be realized through a series of action steps. The appendix at the end of this book offers many other ways for moving goals into successful outcomes.

Questions

1. What process is followed in your parish to move goals into action, or if none, what changes would have to be made to make this happen?

2. What actions would you like to see formulated for the area of the parish in which you are most active?

Section Four

The Art and Science of Parish Leadership

What does the Lord require of you
but to do justice, and to love kindness,
and to walk humbly with your God?

— Micah 6:8

There is both an art to leading a parish and a science. The art is the intuitive, sensitive side of sizing up a situation and knowing deep within what is the right course of action to follow, what are the good decisions to make. This is the side of leading that keeps holding up the mission and dream so that they are not forgotten or put aside when choices are made. It is the art of leading that gently challenges people to change and grow when they are stuck in a rut or out of synch with Gospel imperatives. This is the part of leadership that hears the muffled voices of the timid, the minorities, those on the fringe who have wise things to say and important lessons to offer. This is the heartbeat of leading.

There is also a science to parish leadership. This includes all the aspects of management, structure, and organization. This side of leading takes place in the head more than in the heart. It plans ahead and is ready for the unexpected, prepared for a crisis or disaster, well equipped for inclusion and participation.

It is, of course, too much to expect from any one person to be able to lead well from both perspectives. Thus the need for partnership and shared decision making. Both thinking and feeling, sensing and intuition come into play, and often simultaneously. Parish leadership is a dance involving many participants and many varieties of music, but it is a thing of beauty when it all comes together.

Chapter Fifteen

What Does the Pastor
Do All Day?

Being a pastor is almost an impossible job these days. Gone are the rewards and perks, leaving only headaches and overwork. People have such unreal expectations. The pastor is supposed to be on the other end of the phone anytime they call, day or night. The pastor is required to respond to each and every email within the day. The pastor's presence is requested at all parish events, at least long enough to say the opening prayer. Add to that the extra burdens of caring for more than one faith community at a time and the responsibilities multiply two, three, or fourfold.

There is a mental, emotional strain that accompanies the physical stress of trying to be in many places at once. Parishioners expect the pastor to be in charge and on top of everything without looking or acting "in control." The "boss" is to facilitate and organize, manage, and lead but never in a manipulative or overpowering manner. People look to the pastor as a model of prayer, the soul of kindness, ready to drop everything and listen, support, understand, solve, direct, answer, celebrate, forgive, grieve, console, and heal. And still people ask, "What does the pastor do all day? He only has four Masses on the weekend and a staff to do the work. What else does he have to do?"

Some pastors, in trying to keep pace with ever-increasing demands, react in one of two ways. One common response is to "take charge" of the situation and personally try to solve whatever problem or issue arises. This is the "I can do it" syndrome. As a result the pastor ends up leading the staff meetings, overseeing construction projects, teaching RCIA sessions or adult enrichment classes, handling personnel conflicts, preparing the weekend liturgies, even to the point of writing the petitions and announcements for the weekend Masses. "It's easier if I do it myself" is the excuse. The drawback is that it lays a heavy burden on the pastor and does little to empower others to participate in the running and decision making of the parish.

On the other extreme, some pastors respond to the increasing workload by withdrawing, both physically and emotionally. They become absentee landlords or mere figureheads, withdrawing from the fray or disappearing from the parish for long periods at a time. One version of this response is a pastor who is not present but still reserves the right to make all the important parish decisions. The pastor's secretary, or someone else on staff, keeps the pastor informed and passes on his wishes and decisions to other individuals and groups. Another example of withdrawal, which is more emotional than physical, is the pastor who is friendly and approachable to all but tends to waffle when people ask for a decision. The main object is to avoid conflict and discord at all cost. With such a pastor, people grow impatient when decisions are put off and no progress is made on important projects and programs.

The best way to deal with these reactions to overwork and unrealistic responsibilities is not to seek a change in the pastor's way of acting so much as to change the system. Chapter 6 suggested that the pastor find a partner, someone who will take the burdens of administration, finance, personnel, and management off the pastor's shoulders. These are skills and duties that do not come with the priestly vocation, are not part of the ordination ritual, and need not be the skills or capabilities of a successful pastor.

One of the primary duties of the pastor's co-worker is to be a "truth-sayer," someone who is not afraid to confront the pastor when needed, telling him things that no one else is willing or able to say. Another aspect of this partner relationship with the pastor is to organize and manage the temporal affairs of the parish, as well as overseeing the operation of the staff and handling other personnel issues. This frees the pastor to handle the spiritual and pastoral aspects of the parish, allowing him time to pray, read, prepare homilies, visit parishioners, counsel, console, challenge, and be present to the parish community. What is most important in this joint leadership of pastor and co-worker is that it be a mutual relationship of give and take where each one learns and gains from the other. This becomes a model and standard for leading throughout the parish community as pastor and administrator call staff, leaders, and people to greater mutuality, inviting them to work toward partnership themselves. Jesus sent out the disciples in pairs. Why not do the same in his church? One reason this culture of mutuality and partnership is so difficult to achieve in a parish setting, however, is because another countervailing dynamic is at work throughout the church. It is manifested in the difference between priesthood and clericalism.

Clericalism

There is a difference between being a priest and being a cleric. There is a little of both in each person who is ordained. Priesthood contains all that the ordained are called to become in the Gospels — foot-washer, servant to the needs of others, healer, proclaimer of the Word, minister at the table of the Eucharist, being the least of all, not lording it over one another. Priesthood is what the pastor is at his best, a person "for others."

Clericalism is the culture that wraps around the priesthood like a tight bandage, squeezing it into a mold that is narrow and self-serving. The clerical culture is not a way of life priests choose;

they are drawn into it even before ordination. It begins with a set of expectations and presumptions that become part of the seminary training. "I'm special. I'm set apart. I serve my people and look out for their needs and well-being. Because I am busy with this ministry, my upkeep and physical requirements are taken care of by others. As a pastor, I am the ultimate decider, and all major decisions go through me. I have a staff to help me with this ministry, but I'm in charge of the parish. People give me respect and deference because of my call to ordination, along with all the responsibilities and privileges that go with it."

This description is more than priests will admit to or even be conscious of, but the culture is pervasive, forcing both the ordained and non-ordained to bow to its demands. The evidence of clericalism is present on many levels of the church today. The return to rituals that emphasize the separation of priest from people, the culture of secrecy that mistrusts the wisdom of the faithful and that helped foster the sexual abuse scandal, the exclusivity in the church of priests and bishops with respect to the people that creates divisions between "us" (the ordained) and "them" (everyone else). These manifestations of a clerical culture keep the priesthood bottled up and prevent it from breaking forth into service and partnership.

But a countermovement is also at play in parishes, one in which the pastor no longer acts alone or is the sole decision maker. Instead, he calls the staff, leaders, and people together to participate with him in discovering what might be the best decision to make or what might be the will of God in the matter at hand. This effort at creating a culture of mutuality is one way that priesthood is freed from the bondage of clericalism.

It is to the benefit of the pastor himself to be released from the weight of the clerical culture. In one parish the pastor was a gifted manager, and most of the decisions related to parish operation went through him. But the parish was not flourishing, and he did not know why. He asked for outside help. In the course of the consultation, it became obvious what the problem was: the pastor himself. To his credit, he underwent a conversion. This included, among other things, a reorganization of the parish leadership that included a council and commission structure described in the previous chapters. A large group of qualified and motivated parishioners now share the visioning and running of the parish. It no longer belongs just to the pastor or staff; it is now a joint ownership with many others working in mutuality with the pastor and with one another.

One morning after Mass a gentleman approached the pastor demanding an answer to a problem he had with some aspect of the parish. The pastor's response was, "Joe, I'm no longer in charge of that area. You will have to go to the administration commission. It is up to them now. In fact, Harold, a member of that commission, is standing right over there. Go see him, and he will help you out." A strange look came over Joe's face. He was dumbfounded by the pastor's response. An even stranger look came over the pastor's face. It was a broad smile of relief and delight. "I did it! I did it!" was his response to the usher standing beside him. "I let someone else take care of it. It's not my problem anymore."

This is an example of priesthood shining through and breaking down the restrictions of clericalism. Here is a pastor who is ministering both "for" and "with" others. Unwrapping the bandages that wind around priesthood is a difficult endeavor. Both the ordained and the non-ordained play into tendencies of superiority and privilege that are the hallmarks of a clerical culture. It surfaces in statements such as, "Father knows best." "Whatever you want, Father." "I don't understand it, but the pastor must have good reasons for his decision." The pastors themselves can be seduced by the benefits associated with this mentality and by the prestige and status that accompany their position. But this is not what Jesus meant when he cautioned his followers to be the least of all, nor is it what Paul modeled by stating, "If I must boast, I will boast of the things that show my weakness" (2 Cor. 11).[15]

Questions

1. What are three things that should be part of a pastor's job description, and why are these so important?

2. How can a pastor get free of the pressures and constraints of clericalism so he can be free to exercise his priesthood, and who are the best people to help him do this?

Chapter Sixteen

A Change of Perspective for the Staff

Clericalism is not an issue for the ordained alone. It can be a subtle trap for parish staffs as well, infecting them in ways unknown to them and causing them to operate in ways just the opposite of what they intend. Superiority and privilege can wrap around their ministry and mold them into the experts, the ones who know best, the masters of their ministry, the ones in charge.

Many staff members get caught in this trap of doing the planning, making the decisions, setting the timeline, evaluating the outcome, and doing all this by themselves. Once the program, project, curriculum, liturgy, or sacramental preparation is planned and in place, then they look around for volunteers to carry it out, to be their "go-fers" in implementing their plans and wishes. When volunteers do not come forward, the staff members complain, "It's so hard to find ministers these days. People are just not as available or willing to be volunteers as they once were. Their faith commitment and generosity seem to be waning."

The difficulty, however, might not lie with the parishioners but with the staff members themselves. What is needed is a change of focus, a turning upside down of their approach, a shift in the definition of what it means to be a member of the parish staff.

Curing vs. Caring

A common experience in parishes is that the staff is doing too much. They feel overburdened while parish leaders and ministers are underutilized. This is not what staff members desire, but in the interest of efficiency and because of time pressures they get stuck "doing it all." A way out of this staff-dominant syndrome is to change from a "curing" way of acting to a "caring" mentality.

In the curing mode of ministry, a person feels responsible *for* others. The dominant desire is to fix whatever is not working and rescue what is failing. In crisis situations, this is an appropriate response but not as a constant behavior. Consider, for instance, a liturgy director who is not happy with what the art and environment committee is planning for the Pentecost decorations in church. The color scheme should be red, but they are going with yellow. The director calls the committee together and tells them that they are missing one of the essential characteristics of the feast, tongues of *fire*. The committee is happy for his assistance, thanking him for his suggestion, but the director senses the members are pulling back and are now letting him carry the ball. He is anxious about this and is growing weary with the way the committee is acting. But at least they are moving from yellow to red. As a curing person, the liturgy director is more concerned with "getting it right" than in how the committee is operating. Without realizing it, he is expecting the committee to live up to his expectations rather than spending time to empower the committee so that it can act on its own. As a result, the director, without ever wanting to do so, ends up manipulating both the situation and the committee to fit his own desires and expectations. He is the one controlling the art and environment ministry. This is a trap that pastors, staffs, and lay leaders fall into without realizing what is happening. As a result the parishioners become passive and unresponsive, while staff members wonder why attendance at meetings is dropping off or people are not stepping forward to fill vacancies.

The sentiments of a staff person who is operating out of a *curing* mode include:

1. I feel responsible *for* others and *for* the outcome.
2. I try to fix or control the situation.
3. I am the protector or the one coming to the rescue.
4. I have a hard time listening to what people are saying.
5. I am thinking more of what I am going to do or say.
6. I feel tired, anxious, fearful, and liable for what might happen.
7. I am concerned with the solution, with being right, with correct procedures.
8. I am caught up with the details and performance rather than with the people.
9. I end up manipulating the situation without wanting to or even knowing it.
10. I expect people to live up to my expectations, to do it my way, the *right* way.

An alternative way of leading is to feel responsible *to* others rather than *for* others. In this mode, the staff person spends time encouraging and empowering others, setting boundaries and limits within which to operate. In the example of the liturgy director, a caring approach would mean that he would call the art and environment committee together to share his concern about the decorations and color scheme. He would listen to their plans and why they chose the colors they did. He would hear it from their side, discovering why they made these particular choices. During this interchange he might suggest an alternative and the reasons why. He might even confront them to consult the liturgical directives for the feast, but he would not take over and control the outcome. He would spend time relating to committee members in order to discover how they view their task and what they want to achieve. He might set up parameters and guidelines, but his role would be more the resource person rather than the one in charge. In this way he shows the committee that he trusts its work and is willing to let go of the process. The liturgy director might even learn to accept the notion that yellow or gold might work as well as red in some aspects of the decorations. Once the feast is over he might also meet with the art and environment committee to evaluate the outcome and assess what changes might be appropriate for next year. As the liturgy director moves from a curing to a caring mode, he is surprised at how well the committee is responding and how much less anxious and nervous he himself is feeling. As a result, the committee works harder at creating a fitting worship environment, well beyond its own and the director's expectations.

In general, the more tasks and ministries that parish staffs can empower others to plan and perform, the more rested and relaxed the staff will feel, and the more resourceful the parishioners will become. The people gain a new sense of worth and purpose while the staff feels less overwhelmed and burdened.

The sentiments of a staff person who is operating out of a *caring* mode include:

1. I feel responsible *to* others.

2. I show empathy toward others.

3. I encourage, share, am honest, and confront when necessary.

4. I am sensitive and listen.

5. I feel relaxed, aware, and free to be myself.

6. I have high self-worth.

7. I am concerned with relating, paying attention to the feelings of the other.

8. I believe that if I share and listen well, the other person will feel affirmed.

9. I am a helper and a guide.

10. I can trust and let go.

The implication of a caring way of acting is that staff members become resources rather than directors, coaches rather than captains, empowering rather than chairing. The person responsible for religious formation, for instance, forms a new committee made up of catechists and parents to plan and direct the faith enrichment program as a group. The staff person acts as a resource to the committee and works with the co-chairs in preparing an agenda for the meetings, making sure the sessions are productive and enjoyable for all who attend. She outlines the job description of the committee, which includes setting up the yearly curriculum, managing the training, preparing retreat experiences, and supporting the catechists. No longer is it *her* program; it belongs to the entire committee.

The principal of the school shifts the focus of the advisory board from one that gives him advice and counsel to one that works as a team with him in setting a course for the school year and solving problems *together*. Based on this experience of being a resource rather than the one in charge, he begins reshaping the faculty meetings so they become experiences of shared decision making and joint ownership. Faculty members are at first uncertain whether they want to invest the extra time and energy this will take, but once they are asked to select their own co-chairs to run the faculty meetings, they begin to become interested and start buying into this new way of operating. Rather than losing authority as the principal, he discovers he has gained more respect and status, not only among the teachers but with the parents as well.

The staff person responsible for pastoral care picks up on this new way of operating. She realizes that in subtle ways those visiting the sick and needy are, in fact, working *for* her rather than *with* her. She forms an organizing committee to handle the recruitment, training, and scheduling of visitors to the sick and pastoral care workers. This frees her to be the resource and support person rather than the one *in charge.* She thought it would never work, but after an initial period of confusion the committee members begin to realize that it will be up to them to keep the pastoral care ministry functioning. She assures them that she won't jump in and rescue any failed attempts. "I'll be there to help but not to save it," she told them. After a few months of the organizing committee's operation, an elderly gentleman in the group remarked, "We used to think we hired you to do all this for us. Now I've come to realize that it is up to *us* to make it work. You are there to hold our hands and give support, but not to step in and do it if we don't show up. It has forced me to be a better minister to those who need assistance, and I am enjoying it a lot more. Thanks for trusting us and putting your faith in our ability to do it. I've learned much more about myself in the process. You're a good leader."

Staff Resource to the Commissions

A good example of staff members acting as resources rather than the persons in charge is the commission structure. The two co-chairs for each of the commissions meet with the one staff resource person before the Leadership Night to talk about the best use of the one-hour meeting. Some of the agenda items that appear regularly include assigning "buddies" for those not present at the meeting so they are contacted soon after the meeting, hearing about each person's connection with one or more groups and ministries associated with the commission, deciding whether any groups need the commission's attention and support or need to be held accountable for what they were supposed to do. It is up to the co-chairs to send the agenda around to all the commission members before the meeting, but the staff resource person makes sure it is happening every month.

Once the commission meeting begins, the staff resource person helps the co-chairs provide an effective and enjoyable meeting for all in attendance. For instance, the resource person encourages the chairs to keep reports to a minimum. Other means can be used to fill in the members about what they need to know, either with handouts or emails or memorandums. Giving reports is a trap that commissions fall into because it is easy to settle back and listen to what is being reported without having to do anything about it. The one-hour gathering is too limited and the time too valuable to be filled up with reports about what is happening in one or another ministry in the parish. Concrete outcomes, action plans, problem solving, and decision making are the work of the commissions, not listening to reports.

In the decision-making area, part of the role of the staff resource person is to help commission members learn and practice the culture of C-D-I.[16] When an issue or problem arises and the commission does not know how to proceed, the staff person asks the group whether this is the commission's decision to make or does it belong to another group. If it is up to the commission to decide, then who are the individuals, groups, or documents that should be consulted before any decision is made? And who should be informed about the decision and the reasons for going in this direction before any implementation happens? As a full-fledged member of the commission, the staff person can call others to exercise this approach to decision making whenever appropriate.

Toward the end of the hourlong meeting, the staff person encourages the co-chairs to assign someone to give the two-minute report to the total assembly and makes sure the representatives to the pastoral council write up a short paragraph of what happened at the meeting. This written report will be part of the minutes from the Leadership Night's activity that will be published in the parish bulletin and on the website for all parishioners to read so they can learn what the leadership is doing.

After the two-minute reports take place, the staff resource makes arrangements to meet with the co-chairs to evaluate how well the meeting went and talk about areas that could be improved for the next one. The sooner this brief assessment takes place the better, possibly either during or immediately following the social that follows the meeting. Paying attention to what worked or didn't work is a way of maintaining quality meeting time together and making sure that the members will be interested in returning to the next meeting. This way of working with the co-chairs before, during, and after the commission meeting is an example of being responsible *to* others — providing insight, encouragement, and support — rather than *for* others — taking over and doing these tasks on one's own.

One other aspect of the staff resource person's role is important. Once or twice a month, all five staff members, along with the pastor, meet to discuss the commissions and their own responsibilities as resource people. Not all commissions will be at the same level of effectiveness or operational efficiency. One or another might be flourishing while another is floundering. Staff members learn from each other what is going well and what needs attention. When a commission is functioning poorly, staff resource persons can help assess what might be missing and what more is needed. Is the agenda prepared beforehand? Do the co-chairs know their jobs? Are they working well together? Is the one-hour meeting time used to the best advantage? Are reports kept to a minimum? Are conflicts handled well? Do missing members have a buddy? Are action steps for working on the goal well defined and within reasonable bounds? Does the commission funnel tasks to other committees or ministries and not try to do the implementing on their own? These are some of the questions staff resource people ask each other to make sure the commission members are working well together and are accomplishing what they set out to do.

The experience of being a resource to the commissions is a good model for other staff members to emulate. Each person on staff is to be a resource to other groups and ministries for which they are responsible. These might include a music committee or a liturgy planning group for the liturgy director, an adult enrichment committee or religious formation team for the education director, a youth core team for the youth director, a pastoral care group or peace and justice committee for the outreach director. All the staff have at least one organizing committee or group for which they are a resource. These are the people who work with the staff person as the co-planners, co-leaders, co-deciders, and co-evaluators. The future is in the group. It is up to the staff members to draw out the wisdom and insight, the ownership and ability, the motivation and energy that lie within the membership of each group or committee.

Questions

1. When were you conscious of operating out of a curing mode and when out of a caring mode, and what did each one feel like?

2. What unique skills are required for being a resource rather than a leader or chair of a meeting, and when have you had a chance to use these skills?

Chapter Seventeen

Quality Meetings
Using Limits Wisely

There are good meetings and even great meetings. There are poor meetings, and there are "get me out of here now!" meetings. But there are always meetings. Even in this era of emails and conference calls, faxes and messaging, there are still face-to-face gatherings of people who come together to solve problems, assess current situations, make plans for the future, share faith, or evaluate what worked and didn't work and why. Some of these gatherings are leaderless. A small group of people gather together to share their wisdom and ideas, to address an issue or solve a problem. These might be breakout sessions in the midst of a larger meeting or an impromptu coming together that does not need the formality of a chair or presider. These small groups achieve their purpose of sharing or negotiating with little need for designated leadership.

For those other parish gatherings that meet with some regularity or that number more than a few individuals, making sure the time together is a profitable and enjoyable experience becomes a necessary requirement if people are going to return for another session. This is especially true for the monthly Leadership Night, at which all the commissions gather.

Leading the Commission

You have been selected from among your peers on the formation commission to be one of the co-chairs for the coming year. The two of you have the responsibility for making sure that the one-hour commission meeting each month is worth the effort and that people find it enjoyable.

In getting to know the other co-chair, you realize how well suited the two of you are for this task. Betty is outgoing and a good community-builder. You are a bit more reticent but a good organizer. Together you agree to lead the meetings alternately while the other pays attention to how well people are participating and whether tasks are being accomplished. The person not leading the meeting would also conduct the evaluation piece at the end of the hour. As a help in your role as a co-chair, Mark, the director of religious education and staff resource person, will offer help and support as needed.

It was Mark who suggested that prior to each meeting the three of you have a conference call to work out the agenda for the night. He recommended a regular time for this call each month so that a routine could be established. Mark also asked that not too much be put on the agenda. "You only have an hour," he cautioned, "so three or four items are plenty. Give people a sense of success so they walk out feeling good about what they have accomplished."

The outcome of the first conference call was that you would lead the first commission meeting and Betty would, as Mark put it, "ride shotgun." As you joined in for the common scripture reading with all of the commissions at the start of the Leadership Night you pray that you can make this meeting a fun and productive gathering for the nine members of the formation commission. "They deserve it," you say to yourself. "There are so many other places they could be tonight and so many other interests to take up their limited time."

As the commissions break into their separate groupings, Betty does her magic of making everyone feel welcomed and connected.

You pass out the short agenda in case people didn't bring their email notice along. The first order of business is to look around to see if anyone is missing. The only one not present is Christine, who is out of town. Agnes agrees to be her "buddy" and give her a phone call to fill her in about what happened at this meeting.

Next comes a word from Mark, introducing Betty and yourself as the co-chairs for the new season. At a special session two months ago, the one that included both the outgoing and incoming members of the commission, the group evaluated what it had accomplished over the year and what goal it would work on for the coming year. At last month's meeting a set of action plans was mapped out for the entire year that would help the commission realize its goal by the end of the year, if not before.

Before taking up the action plans for this month, you begin by asking everyone around the table whether they had linked up with the head of each formation ministry or group and whether there were any issues or concerns that surfaced. As people affirmed that all was going well, Jim, the liaison to the youth group, passed around a calendar of upcoming events involving the teenagers and mentioned how impressed he was with the many activities and events they had planned. He started to launch into a description of what the youth had done in their last social service project. Just then Betty gets your attention to gently tell Jim that this is not the time for giving reports. "Yes, yes, I know. Sorry about that," he responds to your intervention, "but it is so neat what they are doing. It will be in the bulletin this coming weekend."

The check-in of formation groups and ministries continues until Joan brings up a concern related to the Small Groups Project starting in October. "Those in charge are looking for a few more group leaders to head up the next season. They asked if we could help find some people. Here is the list so far," she says as she passes around a handout. "Anyone else come to mind?"

"Ask the community life commission to contact the volunteer coordinating committee for names," one person pipes up. Another adds, "I would like to take a group myself. It's time I get involved in this." A third suggests, "How about those whose term on the commissions was up recently? They might be interested." Joan writes down all these ideas and promises to get back to those in charge of the small groups. By now a third of the hour has been used up.

"Time to get to our action plans," you suggest. "Our goal, you'll remember, is to form an adult enrichment committee that will oversee all that is going on in this area and get the word out so more people are attending these adult formation events. We're just getting started on this. Tonight we have to make up a job description for this new committee before we ask anyone to take it on. I know you've been thinking about it and calling other parishes to get ideas. What have you come up with?"

For the next half hour the commission members are animated in designing the role and duties of the new adult enrichment committee. By the end of the half hour they have constructed a timeline for the committee that includes a set of tasks, as well as target dates for their completion. Everyone is pleased with what they have to show for the evening's efforts. Your job as leader is simple — just keep everyone on track and move them toward fulfillment of the task. Both Betty and Mark are there to offer assistance, but none is needed. The action is finished with ten minutes to spare, and everyone begins to celebrate the victory of the night's work. When the timekeeper comes around to announce that it is time to bring the hour to a close, you and the commission are ready. The person selected to give the two-minute verbal report to the whole group is prepared to do so. So is one of the two representatives from the commission to the pastoral council. He is writing down a brief paragraph of our endeavors to be added to all the other commission reports that will be published in the bulletin next week, along with the activities of the pastoral council.

You then turn the meeting over to Betty, your co-chair. It is her responsibility to invite feedback from commission members about the meeting and whether anything needs improvement. "Good meeting," comes back the response. "We used the time well," a participant remarked. This pleases you. During the refreshments after the meeting you mention to Betty, "Not bad. I think this is going to be a good year for us."

A Checklist for Quality Meetings

The example of a commission meeting suggests key ingredients that would be helpful for any meeting taking place in the parish, whether it involves a committee, ministry, or organization. The following checklist could be used both as a help in running meetings and as an evaluation tool at the end of a session.

1. Don't Go It Alone: Finding a co-chair or partner not only takes the load off your shoulders, it also offers a variety of skills and styles from which to draw, as well as providing checks and balances to the leadership position. Also consider enlisting the help of a staff resource person, not to lead the meeting, but to coach, support, and guide. This addition taps into the expertise and experience of staff members and keeps communication lines open. It also provides someone to fall back on if the need arises.

2. Come Prepared: Make up an agenda or plan of action before-hand and get it around to the participants. If this is not possible, at least make the agenda known to those in attendance at the start of the session. This tells people why they are there, what their task is, and what is to be accomplished. "Come Prepared" also includes the setup of the room. If it is a small group, set up a table with enough chairs for all to sit around it comfortably but close enough so that it is a conducive atmosphere for working together and accomplish-ing tasks. If it is a large group, fifteen or more people, set up the chairs as a semicircle with a focal point in front that helps people understand that those running the meeting know what they are doing. The semicircle suggests intimacy and sharing even though the group may be large.

146

3. Begin with Rebonding: If this is a meeting of people who come together regularly, allow a few moments for people to check in and to identify those not present. Make sure the absentees are linked up with someone who will contact them personally, not just by email, and tell them what happened at the meeting. This keeps everyone in the loop and knowledgeable about what transpired. Otherwise those not present will come to the next meeting and will want to rehash or question what was accomplished at this meeting. It is also important to form links among participants between the meetings, either by email, phone, or letter. If it is a large gathering of people who don't meet on a regular basis or who don't know one another, spend a brief period helping people feel included. For a group of under thirty or forty, a short introduction by each person might be appropriate. If it is a larger group, consider having people introduce themselves to one or two others close by as a way of making connections and bonding with one another.

4. Stay Focused: If possible, a typical meeting should last no more than an hour unless it is an extended workshop or planning session. Much can be accomplished within an hour, but only if those leading the meeting keep it on track. This includes allowing time for personal interaction, humor, and friendly banter but without long-winded speeches, disruptions, and detours. Those conducting the meeting need to allow time for questioning, airing of feelings, and appropriate discussion, all with an eye of leading the group to accomplish the purpose of the gathering within the time allotted. People will return to the next session if they know it will not get hijacked by a few forceful, influential, or disruptive individuals. Staying on course and keeping it well-focused is the hallmark of a quality meeting.

5. Everyone Is a Player: Every meeting has two groups of people, those who think while they listen (introverts) and those who think when they talk (extroverts). The latter need to interact with others and voice their opinions to feel they are participating and taking part in the proceedings. If given permission they will dominate the meeting. The introverts need time and space to process in their own minds what is going on and what they think about it. They need time during a meeting to do this reflecting. One way this can happen is to pass out index cards and have everyone jot down reactions or ideas privately before they are asked to share. Another is to break into small groups of two, three, or four during the meeting so there are opportunities for more people to speak their minds and be heard. A third option is to call on the quieter people, inviting them to give input. These, as well as other techniques, establish an atmosphere of shared wisdom. They help the group realize that everyone present has an insight or a piece of wisdom to share. If someone is not given an invitation or encouragement to speak, then there is a gap in the group's deliberation. As a result, the outcome may not be as rich or fruitful as it could have been.

6. **Timing Is Essential:** A good leader has a sense of when to give the group some slack and when to press forward to a conclusion, when to foster humor and when to get serious, when to invite the group to quiet reflection and when to allow an outburst of ideas and suggestions. Setting a reasonable pace to a meeting assures the participants that tasks will be accomplished but they will also have fun arriving at the desired outcome. Creating a good flow keeps people coming back for more. It is like conducting a symphony that has predictable yet surprising movements and melodies as part of the piece that is being played. In this way, the meeting becomes a harmonious whole to which everyone contributes, but a good conductor is important in keeping the tempo going.

7. **Move to a Decision:** Discussion may be plentiful but only if a decision is made will the group feel satisfied. "We spent a whole hour and got nowhere!" is a frequent complaint. A skillful leader knows when to cut off the information-gathering phase or listing of options and call the question. Not that the group would vote on the matter. This often produces winners (cheers and satisfaction) and losers (grumbling and discontent). Better to stay with the sharing

until it becomes clear a compromise has been reached, a consensus forged. "Yes, I can accept that conclusion," someone might say. "It was not my first choice, but I can now see the wisdom of it." Both resolution and closure are necessary for a group to feel fulfilled. "We got something accomplished this time. We all agreed and reached a good decision" is a statement every leader loves to hear as people are leaving.

8. Pin Down Next Steps: Arriving at a decision is not enough. Don't let people escape without a plan of action. "We made a decision," a good leader will say. "Now who is going to do what to make sure the decision gets put into operation?" This includes a time and place for the next meeting, assignment of tasks with clear deadlines and target dates, knowing who will hold people accountable for what they said they would accomplish. Letting people get away before the details of implementation are worked out leads to poor results. Either the leaders end up doing the follow-up themselves or the tasks are left unassigned and in a void. If and when the next meeting takes place the members will have to start over because the decision was not put into operation. This becomes an exercise in futility and leads to a loss of participation.

9. Bring It in for a Landing: A good meeting has a beginning (prayer, bonding, and agenda setting), a middle (information sharing, arriving at decisions, and spelling out actions), and an end (summarizing achievements and leaving with a sense of accomplishment.) To make sure there is a good ending the leader must bring the meeting to a satisfactory closure. The first rule is try to end ahead of schedule so people are rewarded for their attendance. Second, reiterate what was on the agenda as an indication of all that was achieved. Third, have a capstone ready for the final word. It could be a brief prayer or asking for a one-word summary of the meeting from each person or getting everyone in a circle to sing a song — anything that indicates the meeting has come to an end and there is much to celebrate as a result of the interchange.

10. Check It Out: "How did it go? Is there anything we could do to make it better?" These two questions should end every meeting in order to assure growth and improvement for the next gathering. There should also be a brief assessment by those leading the meeting soon after its conclusion. Eventually a tradition or routine gets established so that all that happens in the parish is evaluated for highs and lows, pluses and minuses, what worked and what didn't. This creates an open system where feedback is encouraged, good work affirmed, and accomplishments celebrated but also where shortcomings, limitations, and missed opportunities are recognized and corrected. A summary of the checklist for quality meetings is as follows:

1. Don't Go It Alone
2. Come Prepared
3. Begin with Rebonding
4. Stay Focused
5. Everyone Is a Player
6. Timing Is Essential
7. Move to a Decision
8. Pin Down Next Steps
9. Bring It in for a Landing
10. Check It Out

Parishes are always limited in what they can achieve — with regard to finances, personnel, programs, ministries, bridging cultures, leadership potential, and so on. Life is imperfect, and so is the parish. But striving to improve the quality of each and every meeting will go a long way to moving the parish to the next level, whatever that may be for a particular community.

Questions

1. Describe a meeting at which many of the ten aspects of running a quality meeting were present. What did you contribute to make it a good experience?

2. Which skills for leading a quality meeting do you have, and which ones will take more effort and practice on your part? Who will help you do this?

Chapter Eighteen

Making Decisions
The Heart of the Matter

No two parishes are the same. Each one is in a unique stage of growth and at a different realization of its potential. There is one aspect, however, that is essential to a parish's growth and development. It is the way decisions are made and implemented. Who makes them and how they are made are two important questions for all parishioners, not just those involved in parish leadership.

Given the present church system, the pastor is the ultimate decision maker. The buck stops there. He is the one in charge, the chief bottle washer, the overall authority. That does not mean that the pastor is the only decider in the parish. Much goes on without his involvement or knowledge. This is as it should be. Most Catholic parishes are too large and complex for the pastor to be in touch with all that is happening. The advantage of the "pastor is ultimately in charge" model of church is that he has it within his power and authority to change the system. He can say, as is happening in many successful parishes throughout the country, "I choose not to be the only decider in this parish, even for the more important issues. Instead, I want to share my authority and decision making with others, whether staff, pastoral council, commissions, heads of ministries, or parishioners as a whole. I do not wish to have the pastoral council, for instance, be 'advisory only.' In this

151

parish I will be one of many members on the council. We will come to decisions together, and we will do this by consensus. If I have a difficulty with an issue that is being discussed, I will speak my mind at the outset and not wait to approve or veto what the council comes up with. I hope that other members on the council will do the same. We are all in this together. We have to work and struggle, deliberate and compromise until we arrive at not only a good decision but the *best* Spirit-filled decision possible."

This is a nice theory, but can it work in practice? Yes it can, if careful attention is given to what is called the "C-D-I" of decision making. Those three letters should be the mantra for every pastor, staff member, and parish leader. They stand for *Consult, Decide, Inform*. The concept is simple but the application difficult. Consider a decision to put a new sound system in the church. The first step in the C-D-I process is to make sure everyone understands the issue, problem, or concern being addressed. It helps to write down the issue or problem so it is clear to all. It often happens that those involved in making a decision have different perceptions about the problem that needs solving. A decision cannot be reached if people have varying concepts about the scope and description of the issue. In this case, after much discussion, those involved agreed that the problem that needed a decision was not *whether* to change the sound system. That was a foregone conclusion. It had been getting progressively worse, and the many attempts at patching up the current system were not working. Something new was required; that was a given. The issue that everyone agreed upon was, "What kind of sound system should we buy?"

Once the definition of the issue was clear, the next step was to determine what group or individuals should be the deciders. Who's the "D," in other words. This is the crux of the decision-making process. Often, when the question is asked, "Who's the decider on this issue?" a number of people will immediately respond, "The pastor."

In one parish, a look of dismay came over the pastor's face when he heard this remark. "Why me?" he asked.

"Because you are the one in charge," came back the reply.

"But I thought we were in this together. I'm not the only decider around here," was his rebuttal.

A declaration of trust and letting go such as this frees the leaders to look around and discover what other groups or individuals might also be the deciders. Some of the likely candidates for deciding about a sound system include the staff, the director of liturgy and music, the parish administrator, the pastoral council, the worship commission, the administration commission, the finance council, the buildings and grounds committee, or even those attending the Masses.

Suppose this issue surfaced in a pastoral council meeting at which the pastor was present as one of the council members. They begin to look at possible solutions. Someone stops the discussion and asks, "But are we the ones who should be making this decision? Does it really belong to the pastoral council to fix the sound system?" "Good point," one of the co-chairs responds. "This is not ours to decide."

Knowing that a sound system touched a number of different areas of parish life and operation, the council members concluded that the decision belonged to a special ad hoc sound system committee made up of representatives from both the worship and administration commissions. Because there were people from both of these groups on the council, those present were able to make up a list of names for the ad hoc committee and determine a timeline for its work. A decision, the council agreed, should be reached within the next three months. "We can't wait any longer on this. It will only get worse, and people are complaining," one council member remarked, much relieved that the issue was finally being addressed.

Notice what just happened. The pastoral council, along with the pastor, decided that it would not be the decider. The body also determined who the deciders will be. This is an important step in the C-D-I process, that for difficult or confusing issues, or ones that affect more than one commission, the pastoral council "decides who decides." Most often it is obvious who should be the "D" for a particular decision. The principal is responsible for the school faculty, the art and environment committee is responsible for what the Easter decorations will be, the administration commission decides to update the parish census. But in those situations where it is not clear who should be the "D," the group at the center of parish leadership, the pastoral council, determines who the deciders will be.

Back to the sound system: an ad hoc committee is formed from names uncovered by the council and commissions. Once this ad hoc committee is given its mandate to decide about a new sound system within the next three months, its first task is to figure out what groups and individuals should be consulted about the best course to follow. Who has the wisdom, in other words, about what is required for a good sound system? Who has knowledge about the best company to hire, the best model to buy at the most reasonable price? It is up to the deciders, the "D," to figure out who the "C" will be, that is, the ones who need to be consulted. The first place to look is the original list of groups and individuals that were considered as possible deciders. These included the pastor, the staff, the administrator, the pastoral council, various commissions, the finance council, and the buildings and grounds committee. Others to add to the consultation list might include other parishes with good sound systems, parishioners who might have some knowledge in this area, diocesan resources, the Internet, even those who put in the current system. In the process, the ad hoc committee accumulates much information about possible systems and the ones that fit within the budget the finance council said was available but still solve the problem of providing adequate sound in the church.

One intriguing aspect about the consultation phase is that those whose opinions are sought often think that they are part of the decision making. The sound system committee, for instance, might have to remind people when they are consulting them that they are not the "D." "Thank you very much for your help on this," a committee member might say to the choir director. "We will take all you said and put it into the mix and see what the best solution will be. Your wisdom and insights will help the committee make a good decision, but the result may go in a different direction from the one you suggested."

Once the ad hoc committee makes a decision, hopefully by a consensus of the membership, then it must immediately make a list of all the groups and individuals who need to be *informed* before any changes are made to the system. Who should be part of the "I," in other words, and in what order? Pastor, staff, council, commissions, and finance council come first. Those active in any and all liturgical ministries might come next. Then comes the entire parish because everyone attending church will be affected by the change. Not only does the committee inform people of the outcome; it also gives them the reasons why it chose this particular company and sound system, how much it will cost, and how soon it will be in operation.

Even after the sound system has been put in place, the work of the ad hoc committee is not over. It has one last task, and this also includes the pastoral council, the pastor, as well as the two commissions most closely associated with the decision-making process, the worship and administration commissions. Within a few months of the installation, these groups need to come together to evaluate not only the sound system — is it living up to expectations and specifications — but also the C-D-I process itself. Did the committee do its job well? Were all the key people consulted? Was everyone who needed to be informed given the appropriate information and the reasons for the final decision? What could be done better next time around? Finally, the pastoral council thanks the ad hoc committee for its efforts, both personally and publicly through the bulletin, newsletter, and website.

The Heart of the Matter

Practicing the C-D-I of decision making is an ongoing process that needs constant reminders and continual conversion. Everyone involved with parish leadership and ministry needs to call one another to task when it is not being followed. If the liturgy planning committee empties the holy water fonts for Lent and fails to inform parishioners about what it is doing and why, the worship commission needs to call them to task for not paying attention to the "I" of decision making. When the finance council makes cuts in the budget without realizing it is the pastoral council that determines parish priorities, not the finance council, then the administration commission reminds them that they have overstepped their bounds of making decisions without consultation. When the staff determines a new way of doing intergenerational faith formation, although good in itself, someone must ask them, "Are you the deciders about this shift? And if so, did you consult the formation commission about it before you made the decision?"

Practicing the C-D-I process does not mean that the pastor can no longer make any decisions. The pastor can come to the staff or pastoral council, for instance, and say, "I think this decision belongs to me. I'll be the 'D' on this one." But then it is the pastor's responsibility to do the consulting of key people before a decision is made. He must also inform others after he has made it, but *before* any implementation takes place along with the reasons for his decision. At the same time, the more the pastor includes others in the "D" of decision making or encourages others rather than himself to be the deciders so that he becomes the "C" or the "I," the greater will be their ownership and involvement in the leadership of the parish. One pastor, after practicing the C-D-I of decision making for a short while, told his fellow priests, with a wide smile on his face, "I don't have to be the only one responsible anymore. Now I'm free to do what I always wanted to do but never had the time because I was so involved in making decisions that others could make. I now have time to do some counseling, give spiritual direction, make pastoral visits. I'm even getting some reading done. Why did it take me so long to figure this out?"

Questions

1. Where have you seen the C-D-I of decision practiced well and with what results?

2. When there is a breakdown of the C-D-I approach to decision making, what can you do to make it better?

Section Five

Adjusting to Change: Bringing Out the Best

If we are in Christ,
we become new persons altogether —
The past is finished and gone,
everything has become fresh and new.
All this is God's doing.

— 2 Corinthians 5:17–18[17]

A parish is more than a mission, more than a structure, more than its leadership and planning. It is people, the People of God. The chapters in this section focus on the parishioners and their struggles in coping with change while still remaining faithful and involved in their parish.

Much has been made of the sentiment, "I may not be going to church, but I'm still a spiritual person." Yes, of course, but how can a parish help in a person's spiritual quest? One way is through services and ministries that provide support and development to the journey. Another is by calling people to ongoing conversion, as well as challenging them to put their faith into action. Stewardship is one avenue to this conversion. So is encountering people who are different from ourselves. This confronts our preconceptions and forces us into a spirituality that is universal and "catholic" in the best sense of that word, that is, inclusive of everyone.

A constant issue facing parishes these days is change. Nothing stays the same. Some see this as frightening and a threat to their cherished traditions and way of being parish. Others embrace change and look on the struggles associated with change as opportunities for grace and new life. It is the task of the pastor, staff, and parish leaders to walk with people through uncertain times and show them what gifts lie on the other side of struggle and change. This is the agreement — the covenant — those in leadership and ministry make with all they serve. "We will be there when you need us. We will try to listen and be attentive, to heal and soothe, to call you to holiness and greater simplicity, to draw you into the faith community and help you feel welcomed and comfortable. We will also challenge and confront you, showing you a way of acting in keeping with the promptings of the Spirit and the urgings of the Gospels. We ask that you do the same for us. It is the commitment we make to each other — to reveal to each other the activity of Christ in our midst."

Chapter Nineteen

A Conversion to Stewardship
Experiencing New Life

My name is Emilio, and I have a story to tell. It all began last year when I stood in the back of church for the 1:00 p.m. Spanish Mass. This was my favorite place to be, one foot in and one foot out of church. I used to joke with my buddies, talking during Mass about our weekend exploits and complaining about our jobs. That has now all changed.

I was born in Mexico twenty-eight years ago. When I was seven years old, my family of ten crossed the Rio Grande into the United States and worked our way north. I loved this new country of freedom and possibility, neither of which I experienced in my younger years. With luck, I now have a Green Card that makes me legal and allows me the chance to find a decent job. A few years ago I met Carmen, and I love her very much, although she is confused about what has happened to me recently. It all began during one of the Spanish Masses.

A woman made an announcement at the end about a little booklet the ushers were passing around to everyone, even those of us in back of church who were about to split. It was called the "Little Burgundy Book," and we had a choice of languages, either English or Spanish. I took the English version, wanting to show off to my

161

buddies that "I'm American now. I want to read English; it will be good practice for me."

I took the little book and stuck it in my pocket, forgetting all about it until that evening as I was getting ready for bed. The first page read, "Six-minute reflections: Stewardship in light of the Gospel of Luke." "Six minutes, that's not bad," I thought. "Why not — what harm will it do?" Little did I know at the time that it would indeed harm me — in a good way. It would "harm" my old way of living and offer something completely different in its place.

The reflection for Sunday of the first of four weeks described stewardship as coming from two Greek words meaning "manage" and "house." "A steward," I read, "is someone who manages some-one else's house, that is, all the owner's possessions." I knew that routine. When I was young our family cleaned homes and offices.

Each night I faithfully read the passage for the day and spent my "required" six minutes thinking about what I had read. Without knowing it, the book was having its way over me. One page made a special impact. "A person may be poor, rich, middle-class," it said, "but all people, to be fully human, need to give their time and skills and possessions to others. We're *made* that way . . . like a rose is made to give others its beauty and fragrance."

I couldn't stop thinking about that. It was like the roses in church on the feast of Our Lady of Guadalupe when I was a kid. I could still smell those roses in December. Each night I looked forward to my six minutes with the little Burgundy Book. As the weeks progressed the six minutes turned into ten and then a quarter hour, sometimes even longer. What was I doing with my life? What gave it purpose? Where could I give of myself?

My girlfriend, Carmen, was starting to look at me strangely. "You've changed, Emilio. I am not sure how, but you're different. I kind of like it, but it's different."

The book ended with some final thoughts. "Taking stewardship seriously, as a way of life, is like the first swim of summer when the water is still almost too cold for swimming. It makes us gasp at first. After the first few minutes (well ... a little longer) you get used to it, and its bracing effect feels great. It is exhilarating."

Now what? I had finished the book. I wanted to do something, but what? For one thing, I now took a seat during Mass and convinced my girlfriend to come to church so we could sit next to each other. She found this strange at first but eventually began to enjoy it. My buddies in the back of church at first joked about me "getting religion." After a few weeks they gave up and just ignored me.

Then came the next surprise. The same woman who had introduced the prayer book made another announcement. There was going to be an "Information Night" next week for those who had prayed the six-minute reflections and wanted to do something about it. Everyone was invited, but it was especially important for those who had been faithful to the daily prayer. This got my attention; she was speaking my language. I was embarrassed to admit it to Carmen, but I sheepishly said to her, "I think I'm going to go. Want to come along?"

"No, not really. Anyway, I have to work that night."

"There's a second option," I urged. "How about that one next Sunday afternoon?"

"No, thanks, Emilio. You go. You can tell me about it."

Somewhat chagrined I said I would. As we left Mass there were tables in the rear with fliers and displays that gave people some idea of what to expect at the Information Night. I stuffed a few of these in my pockets and hurried out of church to talk with my friends and buy some food from the vendors on the street.

That night, because I had finished the booklet, I used up my "six minutes" reading the brochures and handouts. The parish newsletter on stewardship absorbed my attention. It was full of pictures of people, even kids, practicing stewardship. An eighth-grader named Alice had written a poem, a few lines of which read:

> Use the talents God gave you,
>   don't put them on the shelf.
> This is what stewardship is —
>   A devotion of yourself.

"Cute," I thought, but do I really want to get mixed up with this? I don't really have the time for any "church stuff" now that I've gotten a new job.

Despite my resistance, my feet seemed to carry me to the Information Night in spite of myself. The gathering began at 7:00 p.m, and the leader promised to have us out by nine. It started with a short prayer and an explanation of the evening. The group — as I looked around I was surprised by the numbers, perhaps two hundred or more — was going to divide into five areas, and I could choose any one of them to join. The choices were activities related to prayer and worship, including the Mass; education and formation; community life; outreach to the sick and needy; and administration. It was the last one that intrigued me. As the leaders explained each option, the words "buildings and grounds" caught my attention. "I could do that," I said to myself. "I'm good at construction and carpentry."

So off to administration I went. Not many joined this group, about twenty-five in all, and I was the only Hispanic and probably the youngest one as well. I felt very odd and outnumbered. "What have I gotten myself into?" I thought. "I'm way over my head here."

Thankfully those running the meeting put us all at ease, introducing themselves and asking us to do the same. They then explained that there were some openings in administration ministries — I was not familiar with this term — and they needed our help. One by one, those leading a ministry got up to make their pitch. An older gentleman was from the finance council and was looking for those with some experience in money management to offer a hand. I turned a deaf ear to that one. Then came the head of the communications committee looking for those good at graphic arts, computers, website design, or marketing. "Nope to that one as well," I said under my breath. Then the woman who had introduced the Burgundy Books at church stood up. She was on the stewardship committee. I was glad she was there because I wanted to thank her for what she had done to get me praying each day. I did have a chance to do that at the end of the evening, but for the moment she was asking for volunteers to be on the stewardship committee. That was not my gift either — getting up before a group of people. No thanks!

Then a younger man stood up and described what his group did for the parish. "We keep the parish campus in good shape and looking beautiful," he explained. I listened intently to his presentation and asked for a job description sheet as he passed them out to the group. A few others took a sheet as well.

When I looked it over, I was happy with what I read. "This ministry amounted to one Saturday morning a month doing odd jobs around parish buildings and grounds, always with a team of workers. Breakfast is supplied at the beginning and lunch at the end." Who could beat that? I was sold. I signed the sheet, added my address and phone and turned it back in, saying as I did so, "When and where do I begin?"

"Right here. You can join us next Saturday at 8:00," came back the reply. That was three months ago, and I'm still having a ball. Our work team of five guys and one woman do odd jobs and keep the place in good shape. I've been able to put my landscaping experience to good use. I've also learned a lot in the process. I've not missed a Saturday morning since I signed up.

That's not the end of my story. There's more. Some of the passages in the Burgundy Book — ones I keep going back to — talked about "giving off the top." The money I earned isn't all mine; everything is a gift from God. How well was I sharing it with others? Not very well, I had to admit. I put my usual dollar or two in the collection as it came around, but didn't plan ahead about what I would give. Whatever I had in my pockets at the time went into the basket. It certainly was not a "portion of my income" mentioned in the prayer book.

Then one Sunday the "Stewardship Lady" made an announcement about doing something for yourself that you will never regret. "Listen closely," she said. "It could change your life." This I did because she had already introduced me to the two things I thought I would never do — pray each night and get involved in a parish ministry. Now she seemed to look me straight in the eye and say, "Emilio, give some of what you have received." She had me; I was hooked.

"Look at your paycheck," she went on. "Look at your hourly wage — before taxes and retirement and insurance and all the other deductions. What do you make each hour? Now tomorrow morning, the first day of the workweek, the first two hours go back to God. Whatever you make from eight to ten, or nine to eleven, or whenever you start work, the wages for those two hours belong to God. The money is not yours, it's God's. After that, the other thirty-eight or more hours of your workweek are yours. Do what you want with them, but the first two hours go back to God — right off the top."

As soon as she said "off the top" I knew what I had to do. I was now making $25 an hour, a sum unthinkable when our family came to America over twenty years ago. Then and there I made up my mind to give $50 a week to God. That was a long way from what I had been giving but I thought to myself, "That's the least I can do for the experience of these last three months." As the collection came around, instead of just dropping the cash in, I took an envelope that was in the pew, wrote my name on it with a pledge of $50 a week, stuck the bills inside, and plunked it in the basket. I had never given away that much of my salary before, and I wondered if I could stick to it. But I was also surprised at my reaction. I actually felt happy that I was doing it. "This is the right thing to do," I said to myself. "It doesn't matter what the parish does with it, help out those who really need it, maybe get some new tools for our buildings and grounds team, but it makes a difference to *me* that I am able to do this. As the prayer book said, "Stewardship is more than money; it's a way of life." Now I know from my own experience that this is so. Carmen thinks I'm crazy, but I just have to do it.

Stewardship Made Simple

Emilio kept to his word and eventually joined the administration commission as a parish leader. He became a model and inspiration to others to do the same. "Take a risk," he kept telling his friends and family. "It's a chance to do something that really counts."

This story exemplifies the three aspects of the conversion to stewardship: praying, getting involved, and giving "off the top." It is such a simple concept, just this: pray, get involved, give off the top. God keeps trying to enter into a relationship with us, to share both life and happiness. It is up to us to accept the offer and then give back what we have, including the precious commodity of our time, the abilities and skills we possess, and the monetary results from our livelihood. Sharing the blessing we have received is a given; being a Christian demands it. The parish provides a framework and the outlets for this to happen. The role of the parish is to help people realize and fulfill their stewardship aspirations.

The first step toward an awareness of stewardship is a commitment to prayer. During Lent, or at some other time throughout the year, the stewardship committee might invite people to make a commitment to pray each day for at least six minutes. Everyone is encouraged to find a regular place and time for prayer. The committee would provide helps and guides about how to pray, along with materials and scripture passages as resources. One example is the "Little Burgundy Book" initiated by the late Bishop Kenneth Untener and available through the Diocese of Saginaw.[18] Whatever resource is used, prayer is the beginning of good stewardship.

Before sharing one's talents or treasure comes a commitment to daily prayer. Everything else flows from this.

The next step is a commitment to become involved in at least one ministry or service project, either sponsored by the parish or some other outlet. Many commitments and activities fill people's lives, but these are usually connected to family and friends. What stewardship asks is to get involved in something new and different, something apostolic and renewing. Everyone has a cluster of skills and resources that might benefit others. The parish provides an outlet for sharing these abilities. The stewardship committee, working in conjunction with the volunteer coordinating committee, begins by discovering what options for involvement exist in the areas of worship, community life, formation, outreach, or administrative services, as well as other opportunities outside the parish.[19] Once the tasks and ministries are identified, people are personally invited to an Information Night to learn what is needed and what area might be of interest to them. The expectation is that each person chooses one ministry or activity for the coming year, something outside that person's regular circle of personal and family activities. This is a commitment to use a talent in a new way, a chance to try out one's abilities in a new activity. Everyone who comes to the Information Night learns what is available and makes a commitment to an activity or ministry for the remainder of the year.

Finally, after committing to daily prayer and a new area of involvement, people are asked to make up a plan of financial giving for the year. One approach is to ask people to figure out their weekly hourly wage. Whether they are paid on an hourly basis, a yearly salary, or fixed income, it is possible to determine how much they make each hour of their workweek. If, for instance, someone makes $52,000 a year, then the hourly wage is $25. A salary of $104,000 a year comes to $50 an hour. Each week, the amount a person makes for the first two hours of work on Monday morning goes back to God. Where that money is donated is up to the individual. All or part of it might go to the parish for its ministries, upkeep, and outreach, or to some other worthy cause. Wherever it goes, the commitment is the same; the first few hours of each workweek go back to God "off the top," not what is left over after other expenses and deductions. God deserves at least that much in return for our life and livelihood.

The timeline will vary in each parish according to its rhythm of celebrations and activities. A typical progression might be to ask for a prayer commitment at the beginning of Lent, for getting involved in a ministry or activity in September, and for a financial plan of giving in November. Another scenario would be a more concentrated effort in the fall of each year, starting with a prayer booklet in September or October, followed by a combined push for parish involvement and financial giving a few weeks after the completion of the prayer component. Whatever schema is used, the core of the process is always the same, helping people realize the obligation they have as baptized Christians to return a portion of what they have received back to God, the One who gave it to us in the first place.

Questions

1. What is your own personal commitment to stewardship, including prayer, service, and finances, and how has this changed over recent years?

2. In what ways has the parish challenged all parishioners to give a portion of their time, talents, and treasure back to God, and what more is needed in this area?

Chapter Twenty

Multicultural Parishes
The Many Become One

Sunday morning at All Saints parish begins with a quiet, meditative Mass at 7:30 a.m. It is an older crowd that attends, everyone filing into their "own" pews as they have done for many years. Nothing unusual about that. The next liturgy is at 9:00 a.m., a family Mass filled with young children, lively music, and a responsive crowd. This is followed by the 10:30 a.m. liturgy, which has music led by a large Gospel choir and a racially mixed congregation that loves to sing and make "a joyful noise to the Lord."

Then comes the noon Mass in Spanish. The church is overflowing with Hispanics of all ages and from many backgrounds, representing Mexico, Central and South America, and the Caribbean. As the Gospel choir files out from the 10:30 Mass, its place is immediately taken over by a whole new group of singers and musicians toting guitars, amplifiers, keyboards, and drums. The language shifts from English to Spanish, and the church takes on a different character as the Mass begins. But the Hispanics are not able to linger long afterward. At 2:00 p.m. a new group arrives for worship, the Vietnamese community. The women are dressed in long white gowns, the men in suits and ties. The Mass begins with the congregation responding to the priest in gentle, melodic phrases that drift through the church like the songs of angels. It is difficult for the Vietnamese to celebrate so late in the day but they have made the most of it by having their own religious instruction classes for the children right after Mass. Many of the people participate, even teenagers, as many small clusters of children congregate in the school classrooms to learn about their faith and religious traditions. The Vietnamese community can't stay in church because every Sunday afternoon there are baptisms, lots of them, each Sunday emphasizing a different cultural group.

This is not the end of the liturgical celebrations. At 5:30 p.m., the young people's Mass takes place. Special efforts have been made to attract teenagers from the different cultures with varying success. This liturgy belongs to the youth. They are the musicians, readers, ushers, Eucharistic ministers, and servers. As one teenager put it, "I love to come to this Mass because my friends are there, and we have a chance to be the welcomers and readers and ushers and singers. It has great music, and the priest gets down to our level. I really love this Mass!"

This marathon of Masses happens every week, serving different cultures, ages, and interest groups. Recently the Filipino community approached the pastor complaining that there was no Mass for them, no attention given to their unique customs and traditions. His initial reaction, which he didn't voice out loud, was to shout, "Impossible! We can't do another thing." What he did say was that he would take it up with the staff and the worship commission and see what could be arranged. "We might be able to do something at the Saturday evening Mass once or twice a month. We'll see."

This is not a fanciful account or fictitious story. It is becoming more and more common in different regions of the country. The cultural groups may vary, but the challenge of addressing their needs and desires remains the same. The multicultural parish is not only here to stay, it is growing incrementally. How is it possible to cope with this reality, offering the services and ministries each group requires and not end up with multiple parishes under the same roof? Given the natural course of human preferences, the tendency is to have separate, isolated communities for different language and cultural groupings. The Vietnamese form their own council, the Hispanics have their own socials and fund-raisers, the Filipinos and African Americans do the same, to say nothing of the well-established traditions of the European American parishioners. It ends up as separate worshiping, socializing groups, all operating in parallel as separate entities with little interaction across ethnic lines and traditions. How is it possible to counteract this natural drift and become one, unified parish instead of several independent communities?

Start with Staff

The staff is the key in bringing various communities together and helping them understand and accept each other, seeing the differences as assets rather than liabilities. Good intentions are not enough. The ethnic makeup of the staff must be the starting point. The staff itself should reflect the rich diversity of the parish. In the example spelled out above, the staff should include at least one African American, one or more bilingual Hispanics, as well as Vietnamese and Filipino members, along with some Anglos who are gifted at bridging cultures and drawing those of different backgrounds together. The burden for creating such a staff should not fall on the pastor's shoulders alone. Having an administrator or some other person on staff as a partner with the pastor is essential. The two together look at the composition of the staff and begin making changes that reflect the changing face of the parish. Inclusion and bridge-building should be the constant theme among staff members. Insofar as the staff has its act together and forms a single community out of diverse cultures and personalities, so goes the parish.

This is where someone from outside the situation and the parish is most helpful in drawing the staff toward greater inclusion and acceptance of one another. Regular staff development sessions with an objective, qualified facilitator will help the members speak truth to each other and keep the focus of the staff on the parish as a whole and not on their own individual ministries or projects. An outside facilitator can also help the staff address whatever difficulties or conflicts they may have with one another. A multicultural parish can be a stressful environment unless and until the staff recognizes how blessed they are to be working in such a setting. One of the best ways to celebrate the blessings of a multicultural parish is to have a staff that reflects in its own membership the diverse makeup of the parish as a whole.

Use the Commission Structure

One of the parishes we worked with had a large contingent of Hispanics, mostly Mexican, and a smaller group of Anglo parishioners, many of whom had been members of the parish for many years. It was this last group that contributed most of the money to the parish and held most of the leadership positions. The Hispanics had formed their own council, but it was off to the side of the governing structure and had little impact on important decisions made in the parish.

When asked to facilitate a planning process in the parish, we suggested a new structure that would include both cultures. "We tried that, and it didn't work," came back the response. "We didn't understand each other's language; we couldn't talk to one another."

Our response was that there must be some bilingual people who could form links between the two groups. We also suggested forming common commissions so that both Anglos and Hispanics could work together in overseeing and giving direction to worship, community life, formation, outreach, and administration. Our suggestion was met with skepticism, but they were willing to give it a try.

During our two-week stay in the parish we tried to locate as many bilingual Hispanics as possible, beginning with the Spanish Mass choir members, the Hispanic catechists, and the Mexican young adults group. It turned out that there were many more people who could converse in both languages than anyone had imagined. These bilingual people were invited into the new structure so that each of the five commissions had two or more Hispanics as permanent members, all of them able to understand and speak in English. They, in turn, communicated to other Hispanic groups and individuals so that all were connected together into one parish, English and Spanish speakers alike.

Because members for the new pastoral council were chosen from the commissions, there was now almost an equal representation of the two cultures on the council, something that had never happened before. The council chose the theme, "Bridging the Cultures," as its primary focus. The council then encouraged each commission to reflect this theme in the goals and actions they were putting together for the coming year.

One action formulated by the community life commission was to call together both cultures through a number of socializing events so people could get to know one another. They called it "Free for Alls." Each session was limited to sixty people, not counting bilingual interpreters.

The pilot session began with everyone in one large circle all around the gym. Each person was to pick out someone else in the circle that they did not know, preferably someone of a different culture. They then walked over to one another, shook hands, and introduced themselves. If they needed an interpreter, all they had to do was raise their hands and one of the many bilingual people present would join the group. For the next thirty minutes the two people got to know each other, sharing some of their background and history with one another. At the end of that time, everyone went back into the large circle, only this time those who just met stood next to each other. (Chairs were supplied for those who had a hard time standing.)

Then, with the help of a microphone and an interpreter when necessary, each person said one thing they had learned about their

174

new acquaintance, starting with the person's name and something about the person's life or background. The two people, in other words, introduced each other to the whole assembly. A facilitator kept the introductions moving so that even with everything being translated into two languages, the introductions took less than thirty minutes for the sixty people present. This was followed by a closing prayer in two languages and refreshments that people had brought with them. The entire session took just over an hour, but many of the people stayed behind in order to spend more time with their "new-found friend."

Another action for "bridging the cultures" came from the formation commission. It had decided to sponsor a Lenten Bible Series in two languages. The five weekly gatherings started with a combined gathering of both cultures. The opening prayer included a scripture text in two languages that would serve as the basis for the Bible study. Everyone then got into small language groups to talk about what the text meant to them. After thirty minutes, the small groups came together into two large gatherings, one speaking English and the other Spanish. A speaker in each group provided background information and an exegesis of the text, as well as incorporating the insights and ideas uncovered in the small groups. After forty-five minutes, all those in the two groups came together for a common social and informal sharing. Although there were two separate presentations, the coming together at the beginning and end of the evening, and the same scripture text used in both, made it feel as if "a bridging of the cultures" was taking place.

These are just two of the many ways the commissions translated the council's theme of unity and inclusivity into concrete actions. As for the Hispanic council that preceded the new commission structure, the leaders of the group eventually decided to disband the council and encouraged the members to join the commissions or other Hispanic ministries if they did not feel comfortable or able to speak English. What was once a necessity to maintain Hispanic identity and presence in the parish was no longer needed. The

Hispanics were now part of the main leadership structure of the parish, working in concert with the Anglo community, not as a separate, parallel entity.

This account of how one multicultural parish came together as a single unit has been repeated in many other locations. It is a "both-and" reality. There must be opportunities for each culture to worship and interact with one another in ways that fit their cultural backgrounds and inclinations. At the same time, the various cultures need a framework and planned activities to draw them together into one parish community. This begins with a multicultural staff, a single pastoral council, one set of commissions that include representatives from all the cultures, one common decision-making process, one image of a single parish that is inclusive and accepting of all. This is the mission and purpose that drives both the leadership and parishioners. "We are one entity, not two or three or more parallel groups. We are one community with many hues and voices. We come together around the table of Eucharist, each in our own way. We reach out in service and ministry and companionship to each and every person, no matter one's background, heritage, or abilities. We are one, and no one is excluded from our spiritual family. Come join us; you have a home in us."

Questions

1. List the ways in which all the various ethnic cultures of the parish are recognized and acknowledged as offering unique riches and assets to the community as a whole.

2. How are representatives of the various ethnic groups given a voice in parish leadership and decision making, and what more is needed to make this happen?

Chapter Twenty-One

Parish Transitions

An Invitation to Renewal

Excerpts from the Diary of a Pastor in the Midst of Transition

Feb. 13 — Having Just Seen the Bishop

Am I being punished for doing a good job? Why has the bishop just asked me to leave the parish I love? It's not fair! I've been here less than five years. By rights I should have another seven to enjoy this place. But no, five years is all I get. Why me, Lord? This parish was nothing when I came, nothing. I hate to be boastful, but it's true. Poor Joe had been here way too long; he had let it go to seed. The staff was dispirited and unaccountable, the council was down to a few people, parishioners were doing their own thing. It wasn't easy, but this place has turned around in the last few years. It is finally up and running again. New staff members have been hired, the deadwood and complainers are gone. I have Colleen as a wonderfully gifted administrator. She's my other self, the one who calls me to task when I get carried away with something, the one who picks me up when I get down, the one who shows me how to get through crises and manage conflicts, the one who pushes me out the door for my day off. The council is a collection of real saints. They are so wise and generous with their time, they put me to shame. When all the commissions come together each month, it gives me shivers to see the things they come up with. I'm so proud and excited to be part of this parish. It is almost as if the place doesn't need me; they can carry it on their own.

Oh my goodness, what am I saying? Have I made myself dispensable? Is that why the bishop is pulling the plug, because I'm not needed here anymore? He *said* it was because he needed me at St. Elizabeth's. I know that parish could use a lot of help, but what will become of all the good that is happening here? A new pastor could come in and destroy the whole thing within six months. This place would be right back where it started, only with a ton of frustrated and disgruntled leaders and people. It's not fair.

What can I do — what can *we* do — to make sure this doesn't happen? I keep hearing that scripture quote, "To dig I am not able, to beg I am ashamed." That was the unfaithful servant who feathered his nest before he got fired. I was not unfaithful, so why am I getting canned? What can I do to ease the shock of this transition? Too bad the bishop wouldn't listen to my protestations. But he did say, "I owe you one, Matt. I'll make it up to you." That was nice of him to say, but did he really mean it? I'm certainly going to hold him to his word, especially in finding a good replacement. There aren't many options, but there must be someone who would be a good fit. These people deserve it. I deserve it!

So what are my next steps? If *I* had no idea this was coming, then no one else will believe it either. How can I tell them? What's the best strategy? It has to be well orchestrated so they don't go, en masse, to picket the bishop. Should I announce it piecemeal, first staff, then council and commissions, then parishioners, or should I tell them all at once? The bishop promised me I could do it my way. At the moment only he and I know about this. What's the best strategy? I can't even think straight right now. I'm too overwhelmed and angry. This is all so new and unexpected. My whole world is upside-down.

First thing is to sit down with Colleen and see what she has to say. This will hit her hard. We've developed such a good relationship over the last few years. I will miss her terribly, but thank God she is here to ease the parish through the transition and to break in the new pastor. Whoever it will be gets the best appointment of any parish in the diocese.

Feb. 14 — My Meeting with Colleen

What an incredibly strong and gifted woman. She cried, of course, but spoke such truth and wisdom. She has such good sense. "Call a special meeting of the staff and council," she said. "They are your core leaders. They are at the center of all that happens around here. Respect them enough to level with them, and do it soon. We don't have much time. Lots has to happen before you leave in June." She said this through her tears and sniffles. It was so touching and sincere. "Maybe this is for the best," she went on. "You've given your best here and done a good job. Now go to St. Elizabeth's and do likewise."

The plan the two of us worked out was to tell the staff and council at a special meeting next week. Then call a town hall gathering for the following Sunday. It would be up to the commissions to get everyone there. Before then I would get to the bishop and clue him in about our timeline so he could let St. Elizabeth's know about this change. They should hear it from him and not from the gossip mill. Perhaps it would be better not to say where I was going, although I don't like keeping people in the dark. I'll see what he says.

Feb. 18 — Meeting with the Staff and Council

That was a hard one. I began by saying, "God has a plan for St. Catherine's, but I have no idea what it is." The news was a terrible shock, especially to the staff. We had built up such rapport in recent years. The anger in the room was apparent. "Make the bishop change his mind. We need you for the full term." "What did we do to cause this?" "Why doesn't he like us?" "Can we picket the chancery, get a petition going, send him letters and emails or something?"

After tempers cooled down I assured them that yes, it would happen no matter what they attempted and that by this summer they would have a new pastor. "You can keep causing a rumpus and fight the inevitable," I told them. "Or we can look at this as an opportunity and an occasion for renewal and growth. It's in our hands to make this a time of grace for the parish."

We then got started planning the town hall meeting for Sunday, working out the details for getting a good turnout and strategizing about what would be needed during these months of transition. We all agreed that a special transition team should be formed to coordinate and oversee the process. First on its list of duties would be a report to the bishop and diocesan personnel board about the parish and what kind of pastor was needed. "Don't ask for a clone of me, please," I said jokingly. "There isn't any, thank goodness. A fresh, new perspective and way of leading is always healthy." They didn't agree, bless them, but they got the idea. By the time the meeting ended, the mood had changed from anger to resignation. As I had expected, they stoically accepted the inevitable and started constructing plans to make the transition a good one. As the bishop suggested, I told them I couldn't say what my next assignment would be, but being named a bishop in another diocese was not one of them." Thankfully everyone laughed.

Feb. 24 — The Town Hall Wake

What a turnout! Not only did the commission members show up, so did lots of other people they called and cajoled. "Don't miss it — something important will be announced," read the notice. "We have no idea what it is, but it will be worth being present so you can hear it firsthand."

The gym was full — over three hundred people showed up. The council and staff had agreed to be facilitators for small groups, but the numbers would not allow it. We went to Plan B and had people turn to one another after I made the announcement. There was quite a buzz in the room. Thankfully the council had thought enough ahead to have the new transition team chosen and in the gym. They had been sworn to secrecy so as not to let the gossip mill get started before the town hall.

Those present voiced many of the same sentiments as did the staff and council about making the bishop change his mind or my being indispensable. Once the commotion died down, the council co-chairs named the people on the transition team and had them stand up. This quelled the heated discussion somewhat. It showed people that this was a done deal and that it was time to take steps to make this transition work for the benefit of the parish.

So many people came up to me afterward to express appreciation and condolences that I was overwhelmed. It was hard not to get choked up. It felt as if I were present at a wake and that I was both the one who had died and the next of kin. Many conflicting and powerful emotions were swirling around in me at that moment. These people are so great — I will really miss them.

Mar. 11 — First Transition Team Meeting

It's a good group. They have launched into their task with great enthusiasm and are making great strides. They are reading up on transitions and are sharing their insights with me.[20] Now I know what I need to do over the next few months. How I say good-bye is so important, as is wrapping up all the loose ends so the new pastor is not faced with the kind of mess I encountered when I arrived here. The team is also writing up an excellent report on the parish, complete with a booklet full of pictures and a PowerPoint presentation for the bishop, personnel board, and prospective pastors. The transition team promised to have it ready within the month. Time is of the essence if we are going to find a good replacement.

For my part, I'm looking around at the possible pool of prospective pastors and will make my own suggestions to the bishop. After all, he did say, "I owe you one." I've noticed that the staff is pretty nervous about all these changes. Colleen suggested a day of prayer and reflection as a way for them to talk out their concerns and worries about their own futures here. A wise woman.

April Fool's — The Parish Report

What a masterful job! I am so proud of that transition team. They showed off their presentation to the staff and council; it was excellent! Hard to believe all that has happened in the last few years. They also included some plans for the years to come and what kind of pastor was needed to get us there. It was so exciting that I wanted to apply for the job myself. They all laughed when I made this comment, but it was a bittersweet response. They are doing their best, but it is still hard for all of us to accept the changes this will require. I think it is Colleen I shall miss the most. One of my first tasks at St. E's will be to find a partner like Colleen, even if it is an interim, part-time person. I can't do this pastoring alone anymore.

April 15 — Presentation to the Personnel Board

I was not there, but from what I heard, the transition team knocked their socks off! The team was allowed to present their report in person — very unusual. Even the bishop was present. The team was not pushy nor did they have unreal expectations. From what Colleen told me, there was no sense that even Jesus would fall short of what was needed. Instead, it was a straightforward explanation of the commission structure, laying out the goals and action plans for the coming year based on what had been accomplished over the last year. They tried to show what a dream parish St. Catherine's would be for any priest willing to work *with* others. This was a parish where he did not have to be in charge or in control of everything. When Colleen shared all this with me, she said that the bishop was smiling throughout the presentation, almost as if he had something up his sleeve. This bothers me. He's a sly one, and there is no telling what he has in mind. I had better make an appointment with him and feel him out on this. I don't want any more surprises from him — one was enough.

April 24 — Meeting with the Bishop

Well, that was a dud. The bishop was pleasant enough, but he plays his cards close to his chest. The word is out that I will be going to St. Elizabeth's, but nothing about who will take my place. Time is running out. I gave the bishop my top three candidates for pastor here, and he took the names graciously but with little comment. I also asked for a month's break before taking over the new parish. I'll need some time to grieve and let go of St. Catherine's before heading over to St. E's. I feel I need a year to do this, but he did allow me the four weeks I asked for. I will say good-bye to St. Catherine's on the second Sunday of June and I'm due at St. Elizabeth's the third Sunday of July. The bishop also allowed a little interim period for the place I'm leaving. The new pastor — whoever it is — will not arrive until the middle of July. In the meantime, the priest who is retiring from St. E's will handle the weekend Masses. This four-week interim will give the staff, leaders, and parishioners some time to catch their breath and get ready for the new person. Already the transition team is planning some creative ways for putting closure to my pastorate and preparing people to open up to the new one.

May 13 — Staff Retreat

Less than four weeks left. The parties are beginning. Our annual end-of-the-year staff retreat was pushed up so the staff could be the first to say good-bye and grieve their loss. It was a wild success. We laughed and played and prayed and sang. They did a roast of me that was telling for its accuracy; they know me well. Next week is our monthly Leadership Night, and I suspect there will be more of what I encountered at the staff gathering. Regular business has been suspended, and all the commissions are putting on skits to show their appreciation. I got wind that the council was planning a gift for me, but I told Colleen to tell them to keep it simple and within bounds. I'm not sure how successful she will be. What really worries

183

me is that there has been no word about my replacement. Everyone is anxious, as well they might be. My personnel board contact said it was still in the works. What does *that* mean, I wonder?

June 3 — Still Waiting

My big day is next Sunday. I want to be at my best, but not knowing who the replacement will be is killing me. Colleen is strangely serene about all this. I can't understand this. It's not like her.

The liturgy of departure is all set. The 10:00 a.m. and noon Masses will be combined so I can preside and make it my closing liturgy. This will be followed by a reception, and then the staff and council will take me out for dinner. The transition team is taking care of everything. All I have to do is try to keep my composure, although I have been asked to place my stole on the presider's chair when I leave. It will stay there until the new pastor puts it on when he arrives. I'm so up in the air about all this. It's driving me nuts. One thing is sure; I've had enough of good-byes. One is worse than the next. There are so many people I will miss. Once I get to St. E's, that will be my new focus. I can't be referring back to this place anymore. That makes these farewells all the more poignant.

June 8 — Surprise, Surprise!

Today was the most eventful of my entire life; it even beats ordination. It started out somewhat predictably and ended up in a whole other universe. The Mass went well — great singing, all the choirs combined, standing ovation after my homily. At the end I placed my stole on the chair and was ready to process out when who should come down the middle aisle but the bishop! I couldn't believe my eyes. He was all smiles, shook my hand, and then took the microphone. "Please be seated," he asked. This worked for some but not for the many who were standing in back and along the sides. It was like Easter all over again. "I have an announcement to make," he began. "First I want to thank Fr. Matthew for all he has done to make this a model parish in the diocese, for such it is.

I also want to thank him for his willingness to take on a new parish only halfway through his tenure. He was gracious and accepting of this new assignment, and for this I am most grateful. He has also been hounding me about who would replace him. He was — and I'm sure you all are — anxious that it be someone who can follow his lead and continue it on the path he has laid out for you. It took some doing, but now I'm ready to tell you who it is. If I could invite Colleen Kelly to come up here, please."

I can still remember his exact words and the exhalation I experienced with his next statement. "I am pleased to tell you that your beloved Colleen Kelly has agreed to be your next pastor. The correct title is parish life director, but she will, in effect, be your pastor. Fr. Cunningham, the priest who is retiring from St. Elizabeth's, will be your sacramental minister, but he will be here only on the weekends. Some adjustments may have to be made in your Mass schedule, but it will be a good fit, I'm sure of it."

Then the bishop turned back to the presider's chair where I had just put my stole. "I'm afraid Colleen won't be able to put this on when she takes over next month. She suggested to me that you take it with you to St. Elizabeth's as a remembrance of your ministry here. So put it back on and let's do that ending song so the three of us can process out together." He took my hand and Colleen's and out we walked. I was so proud of everyone — bishop, Colleen, the whole gang. What a parish!

The Aftermath

Fr. Matt took the rest of the month to savor the ending of his pastorate at one parish and to get ready for the next. He was delighted with Colleen's new appointment, knowing it was the right step, both for her and the parish. At the end of his short break he joined St. Elizabeth's with energy and enthusiasm. It was a different community in a different setting. Some of what he had learned at St. Catherine's would work in the new place, and other things he would have to do differently. The staff and parishioners welcomed him with open arms. Some had attended his farewell liturgy at St. Catherine's and liked what they saw. There was no transition team to help ease him into his new pastorate, and there was much that needed to be accomplished to bring new life and energy to the place. He soon discovered a retired parishioner who agreed to be a part-time administrator for six months at no cost to the parish. He had been a manager of a small business and a longtime parishioner, having served on the pastoral council and in other leadership positions. He proved to be a worthy partner for the pastor, someone who could give him feedback about how he was doing in adjusting to his new situation and parish community.

The pastor wrote this in his journal a few months after his arrival: "The bishop was right after all. It was the time for me to change. I think I would have been too comfortable and entrenched if I stayed for twelve years. St. Catherine's is doing just fine under the pastoral guidance of Colleen. I'm getting to know these people at St. E's, and they are responding well. They are eager to learn and want to be a model parish just as they see St. Catherine's has become. With God's help and a few key leaders, there is no limit. Now if the bishop would just leave us alone for awhile, I think we can go somewhere."

A Checklist for Transitions

This fictitious story uncovers some essential ingredients that are necessary for any successful transition of pastors. They apply to other parish transitions as well, with a few adaptations.

1. Set up a special transition team to shepherd the parish through the change, and put the team in touch with resource materials.

2. Attend to the fears and concerns of the pastoral staff. They realize that their jobs could be on the line. Give them as much security and support as possible.

3. Work out a timeline for the three phases of the transition — closure, interim, and welcoming.

4. Make up a report about the parish, including history, the present situation, needs and goals for the future.

5. Allow the staff, council, leaders, and parishioners to give input and to express their opinions for the parish report.

6. Help the outgoing pastor put closure to his pastorate, making sure there are no hanging issues or loose ends for the new pastor.

7. Build in an interim period for both pastor and parish. Allow three or four weeks with no replacement present so the people can let go of one and welcome the other.

8. Plan rituals that help visualize and symbolize the transition. This will ease the pain and anxieties related to change.

9. Make arrangements for welcoming the new pastor with special liturgies, receptions, and gatherings.

10. Have the transition team be the eyes and ears for the new pastor, giving him insight and feedback about how he is fitting into the new environment and how the people are responding to his pastorate.

Questions

1. How well was the last transition of pastors handled, and what would you do differently for the next one?

2. What processes for transitions of staff and other key leadership positions are in place, and what more would be helpful?

Chapter Twenty-Two

Clustering Parishes
Three Scenarios

The Many Become One

Clustering parishes has many definitions. In some locations this means combining two or more parishes into one, either because of a shortage of priests or population shifts resulting in demographic changes. Where once there were many Catholics, now there are few. It makes no sense to have a number of smaller parishes when one combined community will do. Although on paper this makes sense, it is still a soul-wrenching experience for those who have to let go of a lifetime of allegiances and traditions and step into a strange new experience of being church. Some people give up and stop attending church altogether if it means worshiping with "that other crowd" — people they don't understand or accept or with whom they feel uncomfortable.

One town had four communities, each with a unique ethnic identity and history. The nationalities of each one had become less recognizable over the years, but loyalties ran deep in each place. It was time to unite into one, and most of the parishioners could see this. Excellent planning had gone into the process of becoming one church, including rituals of closure, time for grieving, and symbols of new beginnings. At one of the churches that was being closed, the parishioners processed to the "combined parish" with the altar slab from their own church. It would become the altar in the new church. Everyone agreed it was a good gesture of unity, but it was a painful expression of passion and death for many of the old guard. As their own church building was sold and torn down to make room for new development, the wound of loss was hard to bear and long in healing.

Whenever this movement from two or more communities into one takes place, a great deal of planning and preparation must go into this most difficult transition. The essential ingredients of any move of this sort must include the following:

First, the diocese must spell out the reasons for the shift, along with the parameters and endpoints involved in the change. For instance, rather than declaring that one or another parish will be closed and combined with another, an approach that holds more promise of success is to spell out the circumstances leading to a combination of parishes and let those involved determine what would be the best path to follow to reach the desired outcome. Trust the people's wisdom and good sense; they will discover a way to make it work.

For example, one way of proceeding is to call the pastors, staffs, and councils of all the parishes together to lay out the situation. "By this time next year you will have only one priest. You will need to determine what should be the one place for liturgy. You will have to figure out what will be the site for the one parish and what is to happen to the other buildings and properties."

The initial response will almost always be, "They can do what they will, but they are not going to close *our* church! Let those others close and have everyone come to our place. It's clear that ours is the one to save; it's better than all the others."

Getting through this first stage of denial and bargaining takes time and effort. Eventually people do move beyond this resistance to acceptance of what makes the most sense if given time to grieve and the freedom to be part of the decision for their own future.

Second, a special planning committee needs to be formed that is made up of staff, council, and lay leaders from each parish involved in the clustering, along with liaison people from the diocese. This committee needs a mandate, a realistic timeline with defined deadlines, and the authority to make decisions. Using the C-D-I process described in chapter 18, the planning committee is the decider, but only after consulting with the bishop, diocesan personnel, and other parishes that have gone through a similar transition, as well as with the parishioners from each of the communities involved.

Broad consultation is critical. What options do we have? What have other places done? Should we build a new church or use an existing parish? If so, which one? Should we come up with a new name? How can we find a solution in which everyone has to give a little so there are no winners or losers?

These questions, and so many others like them, must be raised and answered as well as possible. The desired outcome is to present to the people a possible solution, along with the reasons why this one was chosen. But the parishioners also must be assured that no decision will be reached until a thorough discernment process takes place.

This is the third step in the process: to ask the folks for their wisdom and insights. This happens at each parish community, asking people whether or not they could accept the tentative solution presented to them, as well as the reasons for their response. This is not a vote but an exploration of feelings and reactions.

The result of this discernment goes to the committee to make changes and adaptations to the proposal and then come to a final deliberation of the best path to follow. Once they have arrived at a decision, the result goes first to the bishop for his ratification and then to all those affected by the plan, along with how and when the decision will be implemented.[21]

In one diocese, the planning committee accepted the suggestion of the parishioners that the new combined parish be named St. Jude's, the saint of impossible causes. This was a not-too-subtle reaction from those who were angry with the change. The bishop accepted their suggestion but added the name of a second saint to make it SS. Simon and Jude in order to lessen the impact and still attend to the people's feelings.

Once the clustering plan is determined, the next and most essential step is to plan rituals of transition so that all of the various worshiping communities are included, respected, and represented in the movement to one parish. This is critical, to link the change with the paschal mystery of Jesus — passion, death, *and* resurrection. "Something good will come of all this" should be the underlying sentiment. "There is new life and promise in the midst of this pain and loss." As St. Paul writes in Second Corinthians, "The past is finished and gone, everything has become fresh and new" (2 Cor. 5). This future promise must remain continually in the forefront. Key individuals who are positive motivators should be chosen for this important ministry of compassion but also of encouragement, optimism, and possibility. All is not lost. The new reality, while not the same as the old, has benefits and assets not possible with the old structures and ways of operating.

Finally, after the move has been made and people are being encouraged to "move on" to a new future, the resulting "unified parish" must realize a new ministry, that of being a resource and model to other parishes experiencing a similar movement from many churches into one community. This is not an experience for these few parishes alone; it must be shared. The story of transition from the "many into one" needs to be written down, utilizing vignettes and stories from many sources and perspectives. Give the leaders and people credit for all they have accomplished. Help them be proud of their achievement by spreading the word to others. "We have gone through the jaws of death and have survived. We are a better community because of it. Use us as your source for hope and possibility."

In summary, the steps for combining parishes into one community are as follows:

1. Including the leaders and people of each parish in the decision-making process.

2. Defining the necessity for change and the issues involved in a way that all can understand.

3. Investigating all the possible options, making sure not to make assumptions or limit the alternatives beforehand. Everything is possible.

4. Creating a tentative scenario or possible solution as one of the most reasonable options to follow.

5. Setting up a discernment process that includes all the parishioners, not giving them a vote but providing a way of gaining their feedback, reactions, and insights.

6. Making sure the end result includes something for everyone, not favoring one group over another.

7. Once a decision is reached, providing rituals for closure and transition that allow people a chance to vent feelings, grieve, and come to grips with the loss.

8. Personally inviting those who will be losing a worship site to participate in the transition process, not presuming they are included without direct contact.

9. Not attempting to do any of this without outside, objective, professional help, which means hiring consultants to help you through this.

10. Helping people feel proud of what they have accomplished, letting them become a model and resource to others faced with the same issues.

One Priest — Two or More Parishes

Having a pastor be responsible for more than one parish is a common occurrence as the number of available priests continues to shrink. Sharing a priest is not the best approach to pastoring because the ordained minister is drawn in many directions at once and is often stretched to the limit. For a person who entered the seminary to be of service, just the opposite ends up happening. Because he is usually forced to travel from one place to another to preside at liturgy, he can't stay after the Masses to chat with people, listen to their stories and concerns, or take part in the informal interchanges that are so essential to pastoral ministry. This situation will only get worse until a more satisfactory solution is found, such as a shift in the requirements for priestly ordination. In the meantime, an alternative to being a pastor in two or more parishes is not only possible but even manageable.

The suggestion, which is being utilized in a number of locations, is to have the ordained priest be the pastor in only one parish and someone else be, in effect, the pastor at the other parish. This person may be a deacon or a qualified pastoral administrator, or as some dioceses call the position, a parish life director. Whatever title is used, the reality is the same. Someone other than a priest is in charge of the parish, taking care of all pastoral duties except celebrating Mass and administrating the sacraments. The priest from a neighboring parish comes for Mass, but everything else is directed and managed by the person designated for this responsibility.

If the priest has to preside in more than two parishes, it is all the more necessary that there be an administrator in each location so that the needs of that particular community are being served and the priest is not pulled in too many directions at once.

A pastoral administrator at each parish also provides a structure that can fill the gap in case the priest is unable to "make the rounds" on a given weekend because of illness, pastoral emergency, or while away for a well-deserved rest or vacation. The pastoral administrator can lead a communion service when necessary, even filling in at the priest's parish as well.

This arrangement works best when the pastoral administrator and sacramental minister (priest) work in partnership as a ministerial team. The two are present together at the liturgies so that the parishioners learn to accept and affirm their own leader or "pastor" along with the priest presider. Depending on the custom and guidelines of each diocese, the priest and pastoral administrator may give reflections at Mass, the priest preaching a homily after the Gospel and the pastoral administrator offering insights after communion or at the end.

It is also possible in a given area to have a parish served by a pastoral administrator and a retired priest, or some other priest who might be a teacher, chaplain, or chancery official during the week but presides at the Masses on the weekends. It is not an easy assignment for the priest, but it does allow each local parish to remain in existence and function as a full-fledged worshiping community. This is especially important where various parishes are too diverse to be consolidated into one. Either because of distance, ethnic makeup, or past history, combining into one would not be possible. Employing a pastoral administrator and sacramental minister is an appropriate alternative.

Sharing Resources among Parishes

A third approach to clustering is one in which a number of freestanding parishes collaborate and share resources with one another. This is not a typical scenario in the American Catholic Church. Most worshiping communities operate independently, even manifesting subtle but real competition with one another. The priests may meet regularly as a cluster to work out Mass schedules for the holidays, confirmation dates, and communal reconciliation, but there is little else that is shared in common.

One exception to this pattern was a group of three parishes that decided to stage a common parish mission during Lent. A planning group representing all of the parishes worked out a program for each day of the three-day mission, choosing a theme, designing a logo, inviting speakers, and setting up a publicity committee, as well as arranging witness talks, small group discussions, refreshments, and the rotation of sites. It was so successful that it has now become a regular yearly tradition for the cluster. Such a cooperative effort among parishes is gaining momentum, but it is still a rare occurrence across the country.

As a way of fostering greater collaboration and attempting to break down the competition and "turf-building" among parishes, one suggestion is to plan a "Best Practices" event for parishes within a cluster, deanery, or region. This becomes a special occasion for celebrating what is working in each community and to gain ideas and insights from one another.

This Best Practices event begins with the formation of a coordinating committee that has representatives from each of the participating parishes. The committee constructs a timeline for the process that includes two events six months a part. The first event is a gathering of six representatives from each parish, taking place on a Saturday from 9:00 a.m. to 3:00 p.m. The purpose of this gathering would be to share what is working well in each parish and what needs some help or reinforcement.

In preparation for this Saturday meeting, the leadership in each parish, hopefully working out of a commission structure, would determine one success in each of the six areas of worship, community life, formation, outreach, administration, and leadership. The leaders would also come up with one aspect in each area that needs some help or attention. They would also choose one person to represent them in each of the six areas, along with the pastor and one staff person from each parish to act as overseers and facilitators.

If five or six parishes were involved in the cluster, then some forty to fifty people would be attending the Saturday event. Others could come if they so wished, but they would be spectators or observers rather than active participants.

The Saturday gathering would begin with prayer together as a large group and then people would break into six areas, each with a representative from one of the participating parishes, along with a priest or staff person to act as recorders. Everyone in the small working groups would share what was working well in their parish and what needed more attention. Then, using the insights of what was working and not working, the subgroup for each area of ministry would write up a plan of action that could be used by all the parishes as they saw fit.

For instance, the worship subgroup might suggest a plan for improving congregational singing, or the community life group might concentrate on ways for building up a better sense of community, especially among the younger adults, or the formation group might put together a plan for intergenerational learning that included parents and children together.

All six groups would reassemble and share their plans so the entire assembly could offer suggestions and refinements. People would return to small groups to make changes and adaptations and then regroup at the end of the day for final reports and timelines for implementation. They would also agree to reassemble for a follow-up session in six months to report on what had been accomplished in each parish.

The next six months would be a time for putting the plans into operation. The parishes, using one another as resources and support networks, would begin implementing the proposed actions coming out of the first gathering. Each parish would have its own interpretation of what was to be accomplished, but they would all be working on similar actions and could compare notes as the months progressed.

If the first "event" were in February or March, then the second "event" might be held in October or November. Before the final session, the representatives from each parish would meet together to determine what had been accomplished and what more was needed. At the second Saturday gathering, the representatives from each parish in the six ministry areas of worship, community life, formation, outreach, administration, and leadership would gather to report on what had happened, what worked and why it worked, and what hadn't worked and why not. From these results, each small group would have a chance to celebrate successes over the last six months, uncover what had failed and why, and make commitments to make sure what was put in motion stayed in motion. They could also revisit those aspects of the plan that had not succeeded and determine what changes or new approaches might be necessary.

The purpose of this "Two Event" process is to provide to a cluster of parishes an opportunity for joint planning. They do this by sharing successes, addressing common concerns or issues, and discovering new ways of doing ministry *together.* It becomes an exercise in joint ownership and provides a way for parishes to act in concert with one another in order to achieve successes none of them could have managed on their own.

As a help to "event-oriented" planning for a cluster of parishes, what follows are a few necessary components:

1. Begin with a coordinating committee to oversee the process. Schedule two Saturday gatherings for representatives from each parish. Besides planning these two events, the committee keeps the process going during the six months of implementation between the two sessions.

2. Determine if a sufficient number of parishes "buy in" to the process. At least three-fourths of the parishes in a given cluster, along with their pastors, must be willing to participate in this process. If less than a majority of the parishes participate, it makes it difficult to keep the momentum going.

3. Establish a financial base and resource. Each parish must be willing to give to the financial support of this adventure. The parishes not only need to give verbal support, they must be willing to provide financial backing as well. Other sources of

funding might also be available, such as grants and private or diocesan contributions.

4. Make sure there is diocesan support and encouragement. It is difficult to maintain a planning initiative and cooperative venture among parishes without diocesan backing. Articles in the diocesan newspaper, affirmation from the bishop, support from the priests' council — all these help give this effort legitimacy and credibility.

5. Locate professional facilitators. It helps to have an outside resource to keep this process on track and moving toward a good conclusion. Initial enthusiasm will wane unless there is an outside prod that holds everyone accountable.

6. Remain committed to the timeline. Each parish must see the value of sticking to the agreed-upon schedule of events and deadlines. If one or another falls behind, there must be a mechanism to hold them accountable or ask them to withdraw from the process.

7. Maintain high visibility throughout the process. Use every opportunity to talk up this cluster sharing process, not only within participating parishes but in the diocese and surrounding area. Let any and all know what is happening and how this is utilizing the common resources of all the parish for better liturgy, ministry, and programming.

8. Build in celebrations of victories and accomplishments. From beginning to end there needs to be a continual affirmation of achievements and successes, even if they are only minimal and incomplete. The real benefit in all this is the experience of parishes working together and sharing their resources. Whatever else happens along the way is a bonus.

Questions

1. How is your parish sharing resources, ministries, and programs with other parishes in the area, and what more could be done to foster greater sharing and collaboration?

2. What plans are in place in your geographical area to help plan for a reduction of clergy, and what more could be done to get ready for what changes are likely to occur?

Chapter Twenty-Three

Religion and Spirituality
Still a Need for Parish

A common bromide going around is, "I don't go to church much anymore, but I still consider myself to be a spiritual person." This is an understandable reaction. There is much in the Catholic Church and in local parishes that discourages involvement in and identification with the church. Besides the larger issues of sexual abuse, misuse of authority, the shortage of priests, restrictive regulations, and exclusive attitudes toward women, gays, and minorities, there are discouraging experiences on the parish level as well. Uninspiring liturgies, boring homilies, poor catechesis, and controlling leadership are all too common. As one person wrote in response to our monthly newsletter, "Rote Mass dulls awareness of spirituality. Sexist language angers me and impedes my ability to hear the message. I do not believe that the hierarchy of the Roman Church has adequately bought into the idea of lay participation to offer both leadership training and a real voice to the laity." Despite these many drawbacks, people continue to attend church, longing to find expression for that deep mystery of spirituality that lies within. How can a parish speak to that longing?

Defining Terms

Richard McBrien describes spirituality as knowing and living "according to the knowledge that God is present to us in grace as the principle of personal, interpersonal, social and even cosmic transformation."[22] Religion, on the other hand, includes a set of beliefs, moral behaviors, rituals and a community of persons that "has at least some rudimentary structure."[23] Spirituality is the quest we all have for the mystery of who we are, the discovery of that greater reality that lies within and beyond us. This is a difficult and daunting task. We need help. Thus the emergence of organized religion as a way to capture, explain, and support the mystery of spirituality within each one of us.

Religion is especially helpful during times of confusion, turmoil, and transition. It provides an anchor to our spiritual longing, giving it direction and assurance that we will survive the chaos and period of uncertainty. According to Barbara Fiand, S.N.D.deN., religion is "the articulated response of the community — the gathered people — to the depth quest experienced and intuited in primordial faith." She goes on to explain that the articulated response is "formulated in word (scripture), in code (moral norms), in cult (ritual), and in the worship of the community gathered in prayer."[24] That is the task of religion. Wherever people come together and are looking for inspiration and guidance in their common quest for God, that is where religion is found. It finds expression in the structured response of worship, scripture, and moral norms. But religion needs a spark to keep it alive and responsive to people's inner longings. The freedom and fire and light found in religion come from spirituality. Without that inspiration, religion becomes stale, rule-bound, and fixated. It loses its spirit, energy, and courage to change and adapt. Spirituality, in other words, helps religion stay alive and relevant to people's lives. At the same time, religion gives spirituality a framework and a direction so that the deep longings of our hearts find meaning and articulation.

The Positive Side of Parish Life: Unleashing the Spirit

A Catholic parish, if it wants to be an authentic expression of the Gospels, must have five essential elements: vibrant and participative worship, welcoming and inclusive community, ongoing faith enrichment and development, outreach to the poor and needy, and responsible use of financial and physical resources, all five of which are guided and given direction by a servant leadership. Using these five aspects of parish life as a framework, as we have done throughout this book, we will explore manifestations of the interplay between religion and spirituality. Remember that spirituality is the mystery that lies within, the freeing, creative, dynamic force that is personal and unique to each individual. Religion is the expression of our deep longings in word, code, and ritual, carried out with others in a structured community setting.

Vibrant and Participative Liturgy

Consider a young gay man who was raised Catholic but became alienated from his faith because of what he felt were harsh and unwelcoming attitudes toward homosexuals. His parents, who attended Mass regularly, were accepting and understanding of his lifestyle but were saddened by his rejection of what was so important to them. They knew he was a good and loving person but found it hard that he no longer attended church.

In search of a place where he could feel at home, he decided to move from his hometown in the Midwest to live in San Francisco. He soon found a job and a place to live, settling into a city and community where he felt free and accepted as never before.

Shortly after his arrival he encountered a crowd of people coming out of a church on a Sunday morning. As he went closer to investigate he discovered it to be a Catholic parish. He also noticed that most of those leaving were people like himself, gay or lesbian.

"How can so many be going to church," he wondered, "given how we have been treated?"

He was intrigued enough to go inside and get a bulletin listing the liturgy schedule: one on Saturday night and another on Sunday morning at 10:00 a.m. He made a mental note of this and returned to his apartment. All week long he pondered this chance encounter. God was still an important part of his life, but he had given up on the idea of ever attending another Mass. Now he was not so sure. He had grown homesick after the allure of the city had worn off. He wanted to meet others who shared his values and outlook. By midweek he had made up his mind to give it a try. He would go to the 10:00 a.m., but just this once.

Entering church that Sunday morning was a rebirth for him. As he cautiously entered the building he was greeted warmly by two people close to his own age who handed him a song sheet. The worship space was like none he had ever seen, a church-in-the-round so that everyone was close to the altar.

As the priest entered and the entrance song began, he could not believe his ears: people all around him were singing out loudly and with enthusiasm. He picked up his song sheet and did the same; it was the thing to do. When it came time for the homily, the priest came out in front and spoke words of comfort, sensitivity, and acceptance. This was so unexpected and reassuring that he began to cry. He had no idea how much he missed the words of scripture and the nourishment of the Eucharist. They spoke to his soul and the longings he felt.

From that moment his life changed. He joined the choir, began helping out in the meal program for the homeless, and made many new and lasting friendships. When he called home about this experience, his parents were overjoyed. They made plans to come visit him and see what this parish was like that he described in such glowing terms and that had so changed his life.

Is this a fantasy, something that could not happen in an actual parish? Certainly not.[25] This is one place where religion and spirituality meet, in the Eucharist. Spirituality comes into play on many levels. For the young man, the longing within drew him to the parish. The reaction he felt once he was there surprised and moved him. The ritual, homily, and gathered community connected with his desires and longings.

But spirituality was also operating on another front. The creativity of those planning the liturgy came into play. "What more could we do to give this Mass a lift and new vitality?" the liturgy committee might ask. "Let's get warm and welcoming greeters at every door to invite people in. Let's have the choir act more as a model and support for the congregation rather than doing all the singing itself. Let's talk to the celebrant to see if he could connect with the congregation better." This is where religion plays a part in personal spirituality. It is the organization and structure of the worship experience that gives focus and direction to people's prayer lives, not just during the service itself but throughout the week in personal prayer and reflection, as well as in acts of kindness and service to others.

Welcoming and Inclusive Community

A young priest was given a parish on the edge of downtown Chicago. It was in disrepair and had only a few older parishioners on its rolls. His job was to close it down; it had no future. Instead, he made the rounds of the new high-rise condominiums that were being built in the area. He talked to the young adults who were moving in, offering Mass in the common rooms of the condos for those who wished. He listened to their stories of frustration and competition and loneliness. He invited them to the parish, not for liturgy but for a block party in front of the church. And they came — in droves. The parish is Old St. Patrick's; the pastor is Fr. Jack Wall.[26] It now has the reputation as *the* place for young adults to attend, although people of all ages in and around Chicago flock to the Masses every weekend. Fr. Jack is an unassuming, gentle man of prayer who speaks to people's hearts in his homilies. This has a great appeal among young people who are struggling with meaning in their lives and with the stirrings of spirituality deep within.

Can other parishes follow suit? Yes! What is needed is a genuine atmosphere that "there's room for everyone." Creating this environment takes creativity and careful planning. When a young adult walks by the parish, for instance, does the twenty- or thirty-year-old see others the same age going into church? Inside, does the music fit a younger mind-set? Is the homily relevant to a younger lifestyle? Are there opportunities for the person to meet people the same age and to enjoy conversations about meaningful topics? Another parish that works at including young adults is St. Monica's in Santa Monica, California.[27] The Sunday evening Mass is so full of young adults that a large television screen has to be put outside in the courtyard to handle the overflow. These are a few examples of religion speaking to the hearts of people, strengthening their spirituality through relationships with others and meaningful encounters with Eucharist and sacraments.

Faith Enrichment and Development

People's lives are so full and crowded that religion — read "parish" — has a difficult time capturing the imaginations of people and challenging them to "go deeper." Challenge is the key word. Many parishes do not challenge their people. They expect little and get little in return. To turn the tide, look first at where most of the parishioners encounter the parish — at the weekend liturgies. How can this weekly ritual be formational and instructive without distracting from the worship? Start with the homily. One homilist would often leave people with three letters for the coming week, something they could easily remember and put into practice. For instance, in speaking about relationships, the preacher's letters were A-A-A. These stood for Accepting the shortcomings of the other person, be willing to Acknowledge one's own failings, and making sure to Attend to the relationship, doing the little things that keep it alive and thriving. Another priest had a two-minute "answering" session once a month at the end of Mass. People could submit a question on any topic during the month, whether by written note placed in the collection basket, by email, or by phone. He would pick one and expound for no more than two minutes on the topic. No one left church early on the weekends he did this "answering." This was one way that religion spoke to the spirituality of people's lives and helped them grow in their awareness and understanding of their faith.

Other parishes have given people a single question based on the Gospel reading for the weekend that they could reflect on personally or discuss with their family. Still others have printed out the readings for the coming Sunday so that people could pray over the passage throughout the week. Challenge and depth are the common ingredients in these examples, finding something that will take people beyond the ordinary and routine of their daily lives.

Another vehicle for fostering spirituality as part of faith development is the use of art in all its many forms and expressions. Plays, movies, concerts, paintings, poetry, craft fairs — all speak to a spirituality that cannot be accessed through direct teaching, lectures, or presentations. Those parishes that stress the lively arts as part of an ongoing formation process have more people admitting that their spirituality is increasing. This is the finding reported in Robert Wuthnow's book *All In Sync*. Wuthnow states that "a greater emphasis on the arts in congregational life may be conducive to members having uplifting [spiritual] experiences."[28] His conclusion is: Expand parishioners' exposure to the arts in any form, and their spiritual experience will expand as well. They go hand in hand.

Outreach to the Poor and Needy

The pastoral council decides to "twin" with a parish in Haiti. A delegation goes to that country to make personal contact and evaluate the situation firsthand. The group returns with stories of want and need unimagined by the parishioners back home. The delegation shows a video during Mass that reveals the deplorable conditions in which people have to live. Donations from the parishioners come pouring in. Even children and teenagers pledge their support. A young attorney who is struggling with overwork and finding balance in his life is touched by the presentation. To the great surprise of his wife and family, he volunteers to be part of the group taking donations to the sister parish. He is shocked himself that he volunteered to do this. Something deep inside told him that this would help keep his life on track. The one-week experience in Haiti, as his wife described it later, "ruined him forever. He's a changed man, and this makes me very happy. He no longer is consumed by his work. He has time for us and for others as never before." Taking the risk to visit Haiti changed his outlook on life, work, and family. The parish called forth his gifts and helped him realize his potential in service to the community. His religion, by offering him the opportunity to visit the parish in Haiti, awakened and matured his spirituality. It challenged him to get outside of his own world and to use his gifts, talents, and ideas to help others. He was never again the same person. Just as spirituality is the fire, energy, and creative force alive within each individual and in the parish community as a whole, so religion is the structure and framework that gives spirituality an outlet beyond one's personal experience and worldview. It links the person to a group of people — a community — that is committed to serving others in need. So it is that a group of dedicated people, all committed to a common mission and purpose, can do immeasurably more than a single person can do in caring for those in need and challenging unjust structures.

Using Financial and Physical Resources Responsibly

As the new pastor joined the parish, he realized that the buildings were in danger of collapsing. A lack of upkeep for many years had to be confronted. Rather than dealing with the situation directly, he called a town hall meeting of the entire parish. A large crowd attended, drawn by the chance to meet the new pastor. He divided the assembly into small groups and gave each a clipboard and pen. The sheet on the clipboard contained a map of the entire parish property, both buildings and grounds. He asked each twosome to go around and inspect the campus and then return with their findings. Staff members and school faculty were stationed at key locations to answer any questions people might have. After an hour the parishioners returned, full of fresh discoveries and new insights. "This place is a mess," one person exclaimed. "We had no idea it was in such bad shape." "Besides that," another chimed in, "the land that we could use for a new building would take a lot of work, it's on a floodplain." "We have to do something," a third person offered, "and do it soon." "Really?" the pastor responded with amusement. "So you have discovered what I saw when I first came here. This place is not in the best repair. Any ideas about what we could do about it?"

The result of this mutual investigation and communal discernment was the beginning of a plan to move the parish to a new location and eventually build a new church and school. It did not happen overnight, but it was the beginning of a rebirth of the parish, not just a new plant but a new sense of ownership and involvement as well. What makes this a spiritual experience for the parishioners is that the pastor challenged them to finance this new adventure by increasing their weekly stewardship to the parish rather than initiating a capital campaign. The people responded by increasing their regular contributions each year over the next four years. The parish was eventually able to pay for a new parish center, part of which was used as a church. The parishioners' spirituality was manifested in the new structure, made possible through their generous stewardship of treasure. Could this happen in a Catholic parish? It already has. This is the story of St. Mary's Parish in Derby, Kansas.[29]

Questions

1. In what ways are people encouraged to share stories and experiences about their own spirituality, and how do these give life and energy to the parish as a whole?

2. How do parish liturgies, ministries, and programs foster personal and family spirituality, as well as challenge people to grow and expand their own experience and awareness of the Spirit within?

Conclusion

Taking Parish
to the Next Level

Ronald Rolheiser, O.M.I., in *The Holy Longing: The Search for a Christian Spirituality,* mentions nine reasons why one should go to church.

- Because it is not good to be alone
- To take my place within the family of humanity
- Because God calls me there
- To dispel my fantasies about myself
- Because the saints have told me so
- To help others with their pathologies and to let them help me with mine
- To dream with others
- To practice for heaven
- For the pure joy of it[30]

If parishes could get to that point where people come for the pure joy of it, then they would be speaking to the parishioners' deepest longings of spirituality and church identity. Despite all that drags the parish down, there are moments when it comes alive, makes sense, speaks truth, is an expression of all it could be, and the people rejoice.

This is the Easter experience we all crave, the mystery of new life and rebirth embodied in the Paschal Mystery. It is the same God who raised Jesus from the dead that keeps raising the parish and all within it to the possibility of resurrection and fulfillment. We need to hang on to that hope and belief. As it says in Hebrews 15, "Faith is the assurance of things hoped for, the certainty of things not seen."

The purpose of this book is to give those laboring in a parish, as well as those who long for a better parish experience, ideas and suggestions on how it could advance to the next level, whatever that might be for a given parish community. The movement begins by attending to its mission and purpose — something that can set people's hearts on fire and make them proud to belong to a parish that has an identity and "soul" to it. Those belonging to such a parish say to one another and to all others who will listen, "We are all on this journey together. God is in our midst and calls us forth. All we have to do is say yes to the invitation and give room to the Spirit to work in and among us."

Next comes a structure of inclusiveness and shared decision making so that not just a few are giving the parish a direction and purpose. Many people are offering their time and energy, ideas and talents so that it becomes a joint effort at being parish. The five key areas of worship, community, formation, outreach, and administration are coordinated and directed by groups of people who form networks, assess strengths and needs, set goals, and form groups to translate the goals into action. It is a labor of love that involves many people, all working toward the common objective of becoming a better and more responsive faith community.

Along with a structure that includes many in the shaping of the parish's future comes enlightened leadership, including pastor, staff, and parishioners. "Partnership" and "shared ownership" are the operative words. From the pastor who is willing to enter into an equal relationship with another as a "dual focus," to staff members who act as resources to others with whom they plan and direct projects and ministries, to parish leaders who make sure that all

211

important decisions include a consultative and information-sharing process — these are the stepping stones to a new way of acting for a parish community.

Finally, it is the people who make up the parish, not just those in leadership. The parish is a means to an end, that of fostering mature and responsible spirituality among the membership. This happens by calling people to a way of life that includes commitments to pray daily, serve others, and share one's livelihood through financial giving. It also means opening one's mind and heart to those who are different from ourselves. Reflecting the diversity of the surrounding area by inviting and embracing a multicultural faith community is an important step to a new awareness and level of parish life and operation. So too is the effort at sharing successes and shortcomings with other parishes and churches in the vicinity. Competition never brings growth and holiness, only narrowness and self-centeredness. Just as the parish calls its members to greater spirituality, so too must it undergo continual conversion to reflect God's action in the world through worship, relationships, and service.

Taking the parish to the next level means admitting its blind spots and crying out for vision and insight, trusting that it will receive the gift of seeing what the next steps in its faith journey will be. Rejoicing in this knowledge, the leaders and people step out onto this path that leads to new life. The parish, in other words, is like the blind man shouting out to Jesus in Jericho.

> Jesus said to him,
> "What do you want me to do for you?"
> The blind man said to him,
> "My teacher, let me see again."
> Jesus said to him,
> "Go; your faith has made you well."
> Immediately the man regained his sight
> and followed Jesus on the way.
>
> — Mark 10:51–52

Appendix

Moving from Goals to Action
Seeing Results

It is the little things people remember. Being welcomed warmly as they enter church, someone from the parish visiting a sick loved one, the pastor showing up for a school event, winning a door prize at a parish social — these memories last a long time and shape the image people have of the parish. In chapter 14, the administration commission's first-year goal of updating the parish census was broken down into smaller actions that could be achieved over a one- or two-month period. This appendix will do the same with the goals that were spelled out for each commission in chapter 13.

In that chapter, all of the five commissions wrote goals for each of the next three years. Once these goals were written, the commissions then had the task of taking each one, starting with the first-year goal, and writing up a plan of action that would focus their monthly meetings so that the goals could be accomplished in a timely manner.

In the five sections contained in this appendix, actions will be suggested for how the goals for each commission could be accomplished. These can serve as a model of how a parish might progress from articulating a vision for the future to the realization of a desired outcome through a series of concrete and achievable action steps.

Worship

First-Year Goal: By the year 20___ , everyone entering church for the weekend liturgies is made to feel welcome, parishioners and strangers alike, and all are encouraged to reach out in a spirit of hospitality to others, both during and after the Mass.

Second-Year Goal: By the year 20___ , although ordinarily lasting no more than an hour in length, each weekend liturgy is an involving and meaningful celebration of Word, ritual, and sacrament that is unique to the tone and character of those attending each of the weekend Masses.

Third-Year Goal: By the year 20___ , our liturgies are inclusive celebrations in which both men and women, young and old and those of various ethnic backgrounds, are actively involved in singing and praising God in joyful song.

◆ ◆ ◆

The goal that the worship commission wanted to complete during the first year was to create a more welcoming spirit at the weekend liturgies. This included meeting people as they came in, encouraging them to bond with each other during the liturgy and maintain this spirit of hospitality and friendliness as they left. Among the many ideas the commission members listed as possible ways to increase this welcoming spirit were to have trained greeters at all the doors of church, giving people the opportunity to introduce themselves to one another at the start of Mass, providing nametags one weekend a month, inviting newcomers to raise their hands at Mass, and providing them with free refreshments afterward. Looking over the list, commission members wondered how they could accomplish even a few of these over the coming year. Then they heard in the two-minute reports at the conclusion of the Leadership Night that the administration commission was setting up a committee to do an update of the census. "Why couldn't we do the same?" they said to one another. "What we need is a committee."

At the next Leadership Night, the worship commission worked out a job description for a welcoming committee and contacted two well-organized liturgical ministers to head up the new committee and give it direction. The commission laid out a timeline for implementation and then gave the committee the freedom to accomplish its task. The new co-chairs found others to join the group and, taking the job description supplied by the commission as a guide, began to line up its tasks. First on the list was locating a cadre of welcomers to stand at all the entrances of the church and invite everyone into Mass. The committee called all the ushers together to explain this new initiative in order to get their support and cooperation. When the request for greeters was made, a variety of people responded, including entire families, young adults, senior citizens, and those from different backgrounds and nationalities. Next came an orientation and training session about what the greeters were expected to do, along with a schedule of what liturgies they were to cover and how to find substitutes if they could not make a date. The kickoff was in September. From the very beginning it was well received by the parishioners, mainly because the greeters had just the right balance of friendliness without becoming pushy or overly solicitous.

The worship commission was pleased with this first step toward a more welcoming spirit at the weekend liturgies. They also felt that more was necessary. They decided to launch a monthly "Welcome Weekend," complete with nametags and a chance for people to become acquainted with one another. The commission asked the youth ministry team to have teenagers handle the nametags. The youth were to encourage everyone coming into church to put on a nametag and use it for the initial greeting at the start of Mass and again for the greeting of peace. Also on this Welcome Weekend people had a chance for a one-on-one sharing during the petitions. Each member of a pair would ask the other for prayers for some need or intention throughout the week and would promise to pray for the other person's need as well. On this weekend the refreshments following Mass were provided by one of the parish ministries or organizations. This gave the group a chance to shine and be recognized by the parishioners. The women's club made a breakfast hot dish, the young adults baked cinnamon rolls, and the scouts provided French toast.

After nine months of this emphasis on a more welcoming spirit at the Masses, the worship commission asked for feedback from those attending the liturgies to see if anyone noticed a difference and whether they liked what was happening. The reaction was very positive. As one person mentioned, "I've sat behind the same family for years and never knew their name. Now, after having nametags on, I can greet them by name. We even shared a donut together afterward. It was delightful." Another remarked, "Praying for someone's needs over the month has been special. I try to make contact with the person after a few weeks to find out how it is going. There is a unique bond between the two of us now."

Because the new committee was now taking charge of fostering a more welcoming spirit at the Masses, the worship commission could move on to its second-year goal sooner than anticipated. The focus of this goal was on keeping the weekend liturgies to within an hour's length, except on holy days or special occasions. Addressing this goal prompted a lively discussion among commission members. Some thought putting a time limit on the Mass was the wrong approach because the Eucharist is a sacred action that is too important to be constrained by artificial time limits. Others who had watched people's reactions when the Mass went over an hour replied that no matter what the ideal may be, many in the congregation become antsy and impatient if the liturgies go on too long. They stopped paying attention and began looking at their watches or leaving early. Their attention was no longer on the Mass.

What this interchange revealed was that no group or committee was taking responsibility for planning liturgies, making sure that each Mass had a good focus and flow, and that it didn't go on too long. None of the commission members felt equipped to do this planning. The priests and staff didn't have the time to give it the attention it deserved. What was needed was a small group of staff and liturgical ministers who knew what good liturgy should be and could orchestrate the celebration so that it remained within the desired time frame. The staff resource person to the worship commission was also the director of liturgy. She suggested forming a liturgy planning group to take a look at what was happening during the Masses, as well as paying closer attention to the rhythm and timing of each weekend service. When a baptism or RCIA rite or a lengthy presentation was added, what other elements might be curtailed or dropped? She also suggested that each weekend liturgy be studied for its unique character and tone, with attention given to who comes to each Mass, their age, inclinations, and desires. These insights might result in adjusting each liturgy to respond to the unique needs of these varying congregations. She took it upon herself to do this investigation. She soon discovered that not only was there a recognizable group of people attending each Mass, but that some of the liturgies went as much as fifteen minutes beyond the hour.

This insight was a surprise to all, priests included. It became clear that a liturgy planning committee was needed to fashion the Masses so they had a flow and movement to them that was prayerful, uncluttered, and not rushed but still stayed within a reasonable time frame.

After just six months of work by the liturgy planning committee and the cooperation of the presiders, music director, and liturgical ministers, not only did the liturgies have a better flow, they also ended on time. The parishioners were delighted because there was no commotion in the parking lot, and they gained more from attending because the liturgy spoke to their needs and expectations.

The third-year goal focused on music, especially congregational involvement in the singing. Finding ways to invite and encourage the people's participation in music was the desired outcome. This meant that the congregation would not just listen to the voices of the choir and cantors, but also take an active part in the music themselves. What the worship commission discovered was that all the planning and arranging of music was in the hands of the music director alone. He was a capable person but did not seem to be in step with the more collaborative, inclusive tone the worship commission was trying to instill in the liturgies. Two of the commission members approached the music director and asked whether a representative group from the different choirs and accompanists might brainstorm different ways to include the people in the singing. The director had this as one of his own objectives but didn't know how to go about accomplishing it. He agreed to call a brainstorming group together.

In less than half an hour the group of seven musicians and singers constructed a list of nineteen ways to encourage congregational singing. These included having a sing-a-long one night every other month at which people could gather to sing their favorite hymns and liturgical songs. Those attending would also be invited to sing out strongly whenever they attended Mass. Another idea was to station choir members along the aisles for the opening song as a way of encouraging and supporting the congregation in singing the songs. A further suggestion was to construct a "book of favorites" for each Mass based on input from those attending. These songs, interspersed with newer music, would be the mainstay for that liturgy. A fourth idea was to divide the assembly into subgroups so that the men and the women or the left side and the right side would sing alternate verses. One person in this brainstorming group thought that the abilities and desires of the congregation were underestimated and suggested teaching parts to the music so that the entire church would be singing in harmony.

This last idea struck the music director as worth trying. Over the Sundays of Lent, he taught each of the four voice parts of a song to the congregation so that on Palm Sunday the congregation had a chance to sing all the parts together. They were so pleased with themselves that they wanted to sing the piece again the next

Sunday, a request the director had to deny because it did not fit into the Easter season. But it did become a regular feature during Ordinary Time. The people always loved singing this "special song of theirs" because they liked singing harmony and were proud of their achievement.

This experience eventually raised the overall level of singing so that eventually the repertoire for the congregation included songs sung in rounds, in parts, with special rhythms, and in different languages. The director was delighted with the response, as was the worship commission. The original brainstorming group became a permanent music committee that met on a monthly basis to work with the director in selecting songs and planning music for various liturgical seasons of the year.

Community Life

First-Year Goal: By the year 20___ , there are a number of occasions for people of all ages and backgrounds to come together as a parish community and enjoy one another's company.

Second-Year Goal: By the year 20___ , all individuals and families new to the parish are personally welcomed into the community, are encouraged to make it their religious home, and are invited to contribute to its life and spirit.

Third-Year Goal: By the year 20___ , nine hundred members of our parish are involved in at least one ministry, activity, or project, and thus experience a sense of pride as contributing to the well-being of the parish community.

◆ ◆ ◆

The first-year goal for the community life commission was to provide occasions for the parishioners to come together and enjoy each other's company. The commission envisioned a string of parish socials that would attract a variety of people, both old and young, as well as those from various ethnic backgrounds. Only a few functions now existed, and these were fundraisers that targeted specific audiences, such as school parents, seniors, or an ethnic group. The one exception was the annual parish festival, which drew the entire parish together. But it was very labor intensive and demanded many months of organizing and preparation. Could other, simpler activities be planned that did not require such an outlay of energy but could still pull the whole parish community together?

What the commission came up with was a task group of ten people representing different ages and ethnic groups that would create a string of events, one for each month, with a break during the summer just before the festival. The task group was to decide what events to sponsor. One person from the task group would spearhead each month's event, assembling a special committee to put it into operation.

Once the task group was in place it began by laying out possible events for each month of the coming year, beginning in September. The guidelines for these social events were that they should break even financially but not be fund-raisers, that they appeal to a wide spectrum of the parish population, that they be easy to put on, with no frills or demanding large expenditures of time and energy. Finally, they must have a built-in assessment process afterward by which to judge their effectiveness. The criteria for success would be whether people showed up for the event, whether different ages and ethnic groups were in attendance, and whether people had fun while they were there. The list of events the task group came up was as follows:

September: The September event would be a parish movie night at which four movies would be shown simultaneously. Afterward everyone would gather for an ice cream social at which they could share what they liked about the films. The night would conclude with everyone voting on the films so that one would end up winning the Oscar for the best film of the night, along with Oscars for best actor and actress.

October: Picking a weekend when the color of the leaves was at its height, the parish would sponsor a "Walk in the Woods" event during which people could enjoy the autumn leaves and come together at the end for cider and fall treats.

November: Following Thanksgiving and toward the start of Advent, the next event would be an "Advent Wreath — Christmas Card" activity at which families and individuals could gather in the parish hall to fashion an Advent wreath for the season and start their Christmas card writing. Pictures of the wreaths could be hung up in the gathering space outside of church during the Sundays of Advent.

December: This would be the month for a special Christmas party at which everyone brought an unusual present to be given to someone else at random. That person had to figure out what it was or the purpose for which it was used. Those who guessed correctly would have their pictures in the parish newsletter, along with their unusual present.

January: A Super Bowl/Best Commercials Party would be held, which included not only watching the ballgame but voting for the best commercials as well. Everyone was to bring a small square, unfrosted cake that would be put together as one large cake and then frosted for a halftime refreshment party.

February: A Valentines Party would be celebrated with a special emphasis on anniversaries of any type. The event was to be a romantic evening with dinner, dancing, and fun, not just for couples but for all those in the mood for music from all eras and of all varieties.

March: As a celebration for the feasts of St. Patrick and St. Joseph, the parish would sponsor a "Taste of the Parish" event at which all those from various ethnic backgrounds would bring a sampling of food "from their motherland" to share with others.

April: Following Easter, this social would be an Easter Hat and Card Party. Everyone — men and women alike — would bring a unique hat to wear and show off. Card games of all sorts would be made available for those who wanted to play. An Easter parade would end the evening so people could show off their fashions.

May: As a nod to those celebrating a graduation, this would be a special prom night at which older parishioners would pair up with a younger partner in high school or college, dressing up for the occasion and dancing to music that fit both old and young.

June: At the beginning of summer, when bikes reappear, this social would be a bike trip, with snacks in the middle of the trip and a picnic at the end. The participants would meet at a designated starting point and return to the same place for a common picnic and fellowship. Prizes would be awarded for the best decorated bicycles.

July would not have a social so that the parish could prepare for the parish festival in August.

As the task group began sponsoring these events, even before the year was half over the community life commission could see what a difference these socials meant to the parishioners. Not only were people showing up for them; they were getting to know one another and were pitching in to make each one a success. Not only was the first-year goal being realized; the community life commission was having fun, along with everyone else who was coming to these new parish-wide get-togethers.

The second-year goal was to welcome newcomers and help them feel accepted and "at home" in the parish. Some of this was already happening as recent arrivals participated in the monthly social events. But something more personal was needed. After brainstorming all the possible ways to accomplish this goal, the commission hit upon assigning a sponsor to each new person or family, someone who knew the parish and could show the newcomers around. The welcoming, however, needed more than just a sponsor. After some discussion and creative planning, the commission came up with a three-step process.

First was the need to find out who the newcomers were and encourage them to take an active part in the parish. This could best be done after the weekend Masses because this was usually the first place people came if they were interested in joining the parish. One commission member suggested setting up a registration table in the gathering space with information packets about the parish. The table would be staffed by a "welcoming person" to answer questions and help with the registration form.

Second, once a family or individual signed up, they would be given a sponsor to show them around the parish and be their support and guide. The sponsor would keep in contact for a month, at the end of which both the sponsor and the newcomers would be invited to the rectory for a Sunday afternoon social to meet the pastor as well as some of the staff and commission members. The social, which was step 3 in the process, would include a short media presentation about the parish that described its history, mission, and ministries. The afternoon would conclude with a description of how people could become involved in one of the parish ministries, groups, or organizations.

Commission members were pleased with the three steps of making an initial contact at the Masses, assigning a sponsor to help newcomers become acquainted with the parish, and ending with a welcoming social and presentation as a way of inviting people's involvement in the life of the parish. One of the commission members was so excited by the process that she decided to give over her other ministry involvements to others, except for being a member of the community life commission, and devote her attention to getting this newcomers project off the ground.

She recruited a few others to work with her as a committee, and they set about organizing the three parts of the process: a welcoming table after all the Masses, a group of sponsors to link up with the newcomers, and volunteers to arrange the monthly wine and cheese party at the rectory. The pastor promised to be present at the social, or if he could not make it, to make sure one of the staff members was there to take his place. A fifteen-minute presentation about the parish already existed, one result of last year's anniversary celebration. There was also a welcoming packet that had been mailed out to anyone who registered, but this did not have the personal touch that this proposal offered.

The newcomers committee was pleased with the response it received when it asked for volunteers to be sponsors, to sit at the registration table after the Masses, or to host the monthly welcoming social in the rectory. The committee wrote up a job description for each task and scheduled people for their part in the process. All that was needed were new people interested in joining the parish.

As a way of raising awareness and getting this new ministry started, the first weekend of October was designated "Newcomers Weekend." The presiders at all of the Masses talked about the importance of "welcoming the stranger in our midst." Members of the newcomers committee described the process during the announcements. All the volunteers and sponsors who agreed to be part of each of the three phases in the welcoming process were asked to stand at the end of Mass to be acknowledged. For the weeks leading up to the first Newcomers Weekend parishioners were encouraged to invite people they knew who were not registered members of the parish to come to one of the Masses that weekend and be among the first to be welcomed into the parish "with style and grace," as the announcement put it.

By the time the Newcomers Weekend arrived all was in place. The registration table was festooned with flowers and balloons and signs of welcome. Sponsors were standing by to make personal contact. The Sunday afternoon social was scheduled a month in advance. But would any newcomers show up?

"Yes," was the answer — more than expected. A number of families and individuals, especially among the Hispanics, had never gotten around to registering in the parish, although they had been attending the liturgies for some time. This was just the push they needed. The month of welcoming turned out to be a great success, at least judging from the number who showed up for the rectory party. Their comments as they were leaving, as well as the positive reactions registered on the evaluation sheets, far exceeded the committee's expectations. It turned out to be one of those neglected ministries that was waiting to happen. When it did, people responded, both volunteers and newcomers.

Bolstered by the success of the first two goals, the community life commission turned to its most challenging goal, the recruitment and management of volunteers. The goal stated that over the next few years the number of parishioners involved in at least one parish ministry, activity, or project would reach nine hundred. The previous goals had contributed to this desired outcome, but the parish was still a few hundred short of the nine hundred mark.

Two things led to a recent increase in volunteers. There was a well-defined, concrete need for more parish socializing events and for a better way to welcome newcomers. Second, parishioners were personally invited to participate. Taking this as a cue, the commission made a list of what should be included in any process for recruiting and managing volunteers.

1. Tasks need to be well-defined.

2. People need to be personally invited to volunteer.

3. Whoever signs up must be contacted immediately.

4. There has to be a training or orientation process for new volunteers.

The commission also realized that what was happening now to recruit volunteers was not working. Each fall the parish sponsored a ministry fair after the weekend Masses. All the ministries and organizations put up booths and tables to show off what they did. People were invited to browse and see what was offered and then sign up for a ministry. Only a few, however, took advantage of this opportunity. Despite all the labor and preparations involved, it did not accomplish its purpose. Parishioners were not volunteering or signing up for ministries.

The commission decided to terminate the ministry fair and try a new approach. The staff resource to the community life commission suggested, because this was such a big undertaking, that it would need some extra staff involvement. She confessed that part of her own job description when she was hired as the pastoral associate was to coordinate parish volunteers. Unfortunately so many other duties had been added to her ministry that she had no time left over to pursue this part of her job. Perhaps this new goal on the recruitment and management of volunteers would provide her with the impetus and opportunity to get started on this important aspect of the parish.

Both she and the members of the commission agreed that it would require a group of organizers to get it started. "Help me form a volunteer coordinating committee," the pastoral associate said, "and give a clear job description of what you want it to accomplish. With that I think we can get this off the ground."

The commission settled down to working out a plan for the volunteer coordinating committee. "What if we began by lining up what is needed," one member suggested, "along with which ministries and groups have openings and what those who volunteer will be required to do?"

"That would mean asking all the heads of parish ministries to make up a brief description of what is needed," another replied. This got the commission started. What the members eventually came up with was a detailed checklist and job description for the new volunteer coordinating committee.

1. A simple one-page form is created that ministry heads can use for describing the areas within their ministry that need volunteers. The form should include the name and type of job or ministry, where the ministry takes place, how often it happens, the commitments required for the task, and the skills, training, supervision, and background checks needed.

2. By the end of the summer these forms are passed out to all the heads of ministries and chairpersons of parish groups. They are

asked to fill out one form for each area that needs volunteers for the coming year.

3. The chairs and heads of parish groups are asked to poll their membership for names of people they know who are not now involved in the parish but would be good recruits to join their ranks.

4. They are asked to put the names on index cards and to hand them back to the volunteer coordinating committee by the end of August. This begins the process of making personal contact with prospective volunteers. The concept is that those who are already involved are the best ones to think of others who might eventually replace them.

5. At the beginning of September, the volunteer coordinating committee calls a meeting of all the heads of ministries and the chairpersons of activities and organizations, at which time they turn in their job descriptions and their lists of prospective volunteers.

6. At this meeting, all present receive an explanation and orientation for the upcoming Information Night to be held at the end of September.

7. Also at this meeting, the leaders of groups are alerted that they will be expected to give a brief explanation at the Information Night about what ministries and activities need new volunteers and to hand out copies of the job description to those showing interest.

8. During the weeks of September, letters of invitation are sent to all those listed as prospective volunteers. The letters include which group or ministry submitted their names and why they thought the person would be a good choice for undertaking that ministry or task.

9. The volunteer coordinating committee organizes a special telephoning group to make follow-up phone calls to those

invited to the Information Night, making sure the person received the letter and answering any questions about the invitation to the Information Night.

10. If a number of people indicated that they are unable to attend, then a second time and date would be offered as an alternative. If a sufficient number warrant it, a second Information Night is scheduled.

11. A select group is lined up to offer witness talks at all the weekend Masses shortly before the Information Night, encouraging all parishioners to attend.

12. Sign-up cards are distributed to the congregation on which people could list their own names and the ministry or activity that might be of interest to them.

13. The special telephoning group makes follow-up phone calls to anyone who was willing to fill out a card during Mass.

14. At the end of September all the leaders and prospective new volunteers gather for the Information Night. After an initial welcome and common prayer, the assembly divides into five groups covering the areas of worship, community life, formation, outreach, and administration.

15. At the subgroups, the heads of ministries and leaders of groups explain each area that needs workers and ministers for the coming year. They also pass out the job description forms to those showing interest as each option for volunteering is explained.

16. Members of the commissions encourage every person present to commit to one ministry or activity so that no one leaves the room without handing in a signed job description sheet or at least taking one home to think about it.

17. At the end of the evening, all come together for refreshments and informal sharing.

18. Within two weeks of the Information Night all who signed a ministry form are contacted by the heads of those ministries to thank them for choosing to become involved and to inform them when and where the orientation or training session will take place.

19. Those present at the Information Night but who did not sign up for a ministry or activity are contacted and encouraged to become involved.

20. The volunteer coordinating committee makes sure that all the names of those who signed up for any ministry are added to the parish list of volunteers.

21. Printouts of the new listing of volunteers is then given to all commission members and ministry heads.

22. By the end of October, each of the five commissions contacts the heads of parish groups and ministries to make sure all of the new volunteers have been placed and invited to an orientation or training session.

23. The community life commission also invites the members of the volunteer coordinating committee to a Leadership Night to evaluate the process and make necessary adjustments for the next year.

24. Each month, from October through May, each member of the volunteer coordinating committee calls five to ten parishioners who are not involved in any parish ministry or activity and invites them to consider joining a group or becoming involved in some parish group or function. This might include such simple tasks as bringing a cake or snacks to an upcoming event or helping to serve coffee and refreshments after Mass on occasion. This temporary involvement might move the person into a more permanent commitment.

◆ ◆ ◆

The staff resource person took the commission's outline in hand and assembled a group of ten people to see it through to completion. The new volunteer coordinating committee liked what they saw because it stressed both personal invitations and the naming of prospective volunteers by those who knew that they would do a good job. This showed that people's gifts and talents were valued and needed for the good of the parish community. Getting to the target of nine hundred volunteers would take some effort and might not be reached within the stated time frame, but it was a much better method than the haphazard approach of the ministry fair, and a great deal more respectful of people's inclinations, interests, and time commitments.

Formation

First-Year Goal: By the year 20__, the parish has experienced a revival or mission experience in which at least three hundred people have gained a new spiritual awareness and commitment to their faith.

Second-Year Goal: By the year 20__, there are four hundred adult parishioners from both the English-speaking and Spanish-speaking populations who have a better understanding of scripture and a new awareness of their Catholic faith so they are confident in passing it on to their children and to others.

Third-Year Goal: By the year 20__, there are numerous intergenerational religious formation gatherings that reach at least eight hundred people annually and that foster faith development, prayer, fellowship, and celebration in a communal setting.

◆ ◆ ◆

The formation commission's first goal was to stage a revival at which people might gain a new awareness and commitment to their faith. This would be an event that would spark enthusiasm and lead to greater religious commitment and fervor in the parish.

It needed to be something that would appeal to all ages and ethnic groups, both men and women.

Some of the members of the commission remembered the week-long Mission that used to be held in the parish. They had fond memories of this and wondered whether something similar could be offered now. The commission agreed that times had changed and that a traditional Mission might not be the answer, but something along that line was needed.

"Perhaps we could do a revival like the Baptists, something that will pack the church," one person remarked. "Include a healing service, have a reconciliation ritual, hire dynamic speakers, do it up big. We could bring in the pope!" Everyone laughed at the suggestion, but it served to get the momentum started.

"This might be too big just for us," the staff resource person mentioned. "Let's contact the other two parishes in our cluster. Make it a shared event. Rotate churches, put up a tent, bring in the media."

The discussion got more and more animated until one practical member remarked, "Okay, let's do it. But we don't have all night. How do we get started? Let's make a list of our tasks and lay out a timeline so we can get this thing done. If we are going to invite the other parishes, we have to get the okay of our pastor and council, as well as theirs. Let's start there."

The rest of the evening was spent lining up tasks and assigning duties. "Lent would be a good time for the revival," the staff resource suggested. "How about the third week in March as our target? That will give us half a year to pull it off. We will need to check with the other commissions to see if that fits their schedules. I'll check with the pastor and staff. Could someone contact the other parishes to see if they want to join us?"

One of the co-chairs agreed to do that. Commission members were getting more and more enthusiastic as the revival started to take shape. "What should we call it?" one person asked. After some discussion the group decided to hold off on the name and theme.

They chose instead to form a joint committee involving all three churches and to let the committee settle on the specifics. The commission's task was to spell out the broad outline of the revival so that the joint committee could have a general perception and framework out of which to operate.

The commission agreed that the revival would begin on Sunday evening with the young people's liturgy, followed by a special presentation for teens, perhaps led by young adults. The next three nights of the revival for all parishioners would take place in different churches, each with a different topic and emphasis, and always followed by a social and get-together. Commission members brainstormed possible topics, including "Questions of Faith," "Bridging the Cultures," "Making Good Choices," "Seeking Forgiveness," "Stand Up and Be Counted." They decided that the fourth night could be in the parish gym with a concluding celebration of commitment as people pledged to put their faith into action. An added bonus would be a new awareness and bonding between the three parish communities, as well as people growing in their personal commitment to Christ.

Much was accomplished at the commission's one-hour deliberation during the Leadership Night. Everyone left excited by the concept and motivated to bring it to completion. Each person had a task to perform so that by the next meeting the commission had a strong endorsement from the pastor and the pastoral council, the other two parishes had agreed to participate, and a few people had been approached and accepted the task of being part of the tri-parish revival committee along with volunteers from the other two parishes.

Over the next months the joint committee made preparations for the revival, naming it "On Fire!" They chose a logo and mapped out the theme for each of the nights. The format would include a speaker, witness talks from parishioners, time for personal reflection, and then small group sharing, both in English and Spanish.

As it got closer to the event, large banners and signs started appearing throughout the neighborhood, as well as brochures in the pews, notices in the bulletin and on the website, announcements at the Masses, special mailings to parishioners, radio and TV spots — all declaring, "We are parishes On Fire! Come catch the Spirit."

When the week finally arrived, there was an intense sense of expectation. All three churches were decorated for the occasion. The Sunday evening Mass was filled to capacity, including many young people from all three parishes. A visiting priest who had a reputation for connecting well with young people presided at the liturgy. Afterward those under thirty retired to the gym for their own program, and those over thirty stayed in church for the kickoff to the revival. It began with a bilingual prayer service, and then each language group went to separate rooms for their own program and group process. After an hour and a half, everyone, including the young people, retired to the gym for refreshments and socializing.

This same dynamic continued throughout the week of revival, including common time for prayer, separate language groups for a presentation, witness talks and group discussion, then ending with a social for all the groups together. By the time the final celebration took place on Thursday evening, the people — some three to four hundred each evening — were on fire! They had experienced a reconciliation rite, a time for healing, a challenge to carry the revival into their homes and daily lives. The final event was a morality play put on by the combined youth programs from all three parishes. They had been working on it for the last four nights. It summed up all that had happened throughout the revival and included songs, dance, and skits about how to bring faith alive in one's own life and in the life of the parishes. The formation commission members could not believe what they were seeing. All that they had hoped would be accomplished through the revival was taking place before their eyes, and much, much more. This gave them energy and motivation to start working on their next goal: adult enrichment and formation.

The focus was on helping people learn more about the Bible and about their Catholic faith so they could pass this new awareness on to their children and to others. Thankfully the commission did not have to start from scratch. There were already a number of educational events for adults, including a scripture study course, various talks and presentations throughout the year, and a few small groups that had stayed together after the RENEW program had finished a few years back. But these were all separate and disconnected offerings that touched only a small percentage of the parishioners. If the target was to reach four hundred adults, that would take some doing. Luckily the parish revival experience had piqued people's interest, and many more were now eager and willing to learn more about their faith.

What was needed was an adult formation committee that would construct a master plan for adult faith enrichment and spiritual growth covering the entire year. The first step in forming such a master plan would be to look at all that was happening at the present time and see what more might be possible or desired. The commission began fashioning a job description for this new committee and started looking around for a few people to act as co-chairs, hopefully one person from each of the Anglo and Hispanic communities.

The committee's mandate was simple: pull together all that is happening now in adult education and create a unified, cohesive whole to the offerings. The next step would be to fill in the gaps that were missing. The ideal would be to have at least one presentation per month that would reflect a common theme for the entire year. These monthly events could be sponsored by the parish alone or be held in conjunction with other parishes. Besides these monthly offerings, there could also be special courses on the Bible or small group discussions on other topics held during Lent or in the fall.

Two people were found to head this new committee. One had been on the planning group for the tri-parish revival and was so moved by the experience that she wanted to provide other outlets for those who had attended. The other co-chair had been in charge of the Hispanic Bible study program. She was flattered to be asked to be part of this committee but hesitated to accept the offer, complaining that her English was not up to the task. Commission members and the other co-chair assured her that she would do just fine, so she said yes to the invitation. The two new leaders hit it off together and quickly turned their attention to finding others who could share the task of coordinating the adult enrichment program in the parish. After asking help from the staff and other commissions, a multicultural group of eight people was formed. Their mandate was not only to coordinate all the adult formation offerings in the parish but eventually to reach the goal of four hundred adult parishioners having a better awareness of scripture and of their faith so they could pass it on to others.

The first item of business was to discover all that was presently being offered and take a tally of how many parishioners had attended these functions over the last year. The number was not very large, considering the size of the parish — fewer than 150 people, once those who came to more than one event were identified. Adding 250 new people to this number was an ambitious objective, but the committee was enthusiastic about achieving its goal.

First the committee looked at all that was being offered and found that there were already many options from which people could choose. Doing some rearranging and refocusing would result in at least one presentation every month. For instance, putting the Anglo and Hispanic Bible study on the same night allowed for a common bilingual prayer session beforehand and a combined social afterward. This was a beginning.

The committee then set up a "Questions of Faith" series that would take place each month in two languages, with an inspirational speaker for each group. Committee members wanted to make sure that the participants at this monthly event would be actively involved in the program, both by interacting with the speaker and with one another in small groups.

Once the adult enrichment events had been laid out for the year, the committee turned to the more difficult task of getting people to attend. The members concluded that it was not just the content that would entice people to come but something more subtle. Somehow there had to be an expectation created that said to the parishioners, "This is part of what it means to belong to this parish. It's like coming to Mass on the weekends or attending the annual parish festival. As part of the parish community we strongly encourage you to attend these adult enrichment events as well." Creating this perception and image would take some doing, but there were a few key ingredients that would help it happen.

For example, people might *say* they want Bible study or a talk about their faith, but that will not be enough to get them to attend. Within their own minds they may be thinking, "What's in it for me? Will I appear stupid because I don't know anything? I'm sure I won't know a soul there." Someone else might think, "I've read all about this topic. I don't need to attend. It's a waste of time."

To counter these negative inclinations, the committee began working on creating a positive image for adult enrichment. For the May event the committee put up signs and had announcements in the bulletin and on the website that read, "This Monday night join us for a new way of thinking about the Resurrection. We're limited for space, so only the first fifty who sign up in each language group will be able to attend. The presentation will be less than an hour, followed by a social. The sign-up sheets are in the hospitality area following all the Masses."

The committee realized that no bulletin announcement, no pleading from the pulpit, no poster in church would draw in new people. Personal contact was the only way. So they contacted fifteen people who promised to contact five others. They asked these fifteen volunteers to invite friends and relatives not just to come but to ask for their help as well. "We're having this special event on Monday night" was the proposed invitation. "And we are going to need some refreshments. Could you bring some cookies or cake or something? We'll make sure to save you a place on the sign-up sheet." This personal request for help proved to be a good way of getting people to attend.

Another important aspect about enticing people to attend, the adult formation committee realized, was the fact that it wasn't so much *what* was being offered as much as *who* was going to be there. "If Agnes is coming (or my girlfriend, or someone else from the choir, or the neighbor across the street), then I might change my mind and come as well." As a result, the committee decided to advertise, "Bring a friend. You can stay together throughout the presentation."

Underneath all these efforts by the committee was the realization that the hunger and desire for ongoing faith formation were in the people; they just needed some encouragement and support to take the plunge and show up. This was especially true for those who did not regularly attend Mass. To connect with this large group, the committee not only sent out letters and emails to all parishioners, alerting them about what was being offered; they also enlisted the help of those who did come to Mass. "Come with a friend!" was the mantra, whether inactive Catholics or those of other faiths and cultures. Also, before each monthly formation event, a special tele-phoning committee called fifty less active parishioners, personally inviting them to attend. The homilists at the weekend liturgies were asked to stir up interest in the event, and the parish website offered background information about the presenters and what topics would be covered. Volunteers even blanketed the surrounding neighborhood with flyers alerting people about this special parish function.

This happened each and every month before the adult enrichment offering so that the number attending began to rise from less than fifty when the committee first made the effort to almost two hundred by the end of the academic year. The location of the presentations had to be changed twice to make room for the larger crowd.

The committee was delighted with the response, as was the formation commission. "That committee is off and running," a commission member remarked at one of the Leadership Nights. "It has become a monthly tradition in our household. Even my teenage daughter is coming. Will miracles never cease?"

Delighted with the results from the first two goals, the commission moved on to its third and most ambitious one. The emphasis was on fostering an intergenerational approach to religious formation so that families would attend together, parents and children alike, as well as those who did not have children still living at home. Much progress had been made through the parish mission, as well as the efforts of the adult formation committee. More and more people were showing up for these events. But it was still a common practice for parents to drop off their children for religious education classes and not participate themselves in adult enrichment or faith development functions. A whole new approach was needed.

The commission invited the three staff persons who were involved in religious formation of the children and youth to join the next Leadership Night. This included the director of religious formation, the youth minister, and the principal. The co-chairs spelled out the commission's third-year goal: to foster regular faith formation gatherings for the entire family, not just the children or youth separately. "Was this an unrealistic goal?" one of the commission members asked the staff members.

All the staff responded with wide smiles. "As a matter of fact," the principal began, "the three of us have been attending workshops on just such an approach to formation, and we were about to present our findings to you and to our own committees and boards."

"We're not doing this on our own," the DRE continued, "but we wanted to have something concrete to show you. What do you think of this?"

Over the next half hour the staff spelled out what they had in mind, assuring the commission that they had the pastor's blessing. The plan began with a gathering of the formation commission, staff, religious formation committee, school board, and youth core team. The intent was to explain the concept of intergenerational learning and get everyone on board with this new way of doing faith development. The idea was to have a monthly religious formation "event." For everyone's convenience, there would be three identical events over a long weekend, one on Saturday morning, another on Sunday afternoon, and a third on Monday evening. Each session would start with a meal so people could get to know each other, followed by a common prayer and an all-ages activity to set the theme. This would be followed by breakout sessions for various age groups among the children and teenagers, while the adults remained for a presentation on the theme for the event, followed by small group interaction. The entire group would then reassemble for intergenerational activities. The event would end with a closing prayer, and then people would be given take-home materials as they left. The idea was to have families, as well as other parishioners who attended, reflect over the month on what had happened during the session. Throughout the month there would be support materials in the bulletin and on the website, as well as references about the theme during the weekend homilies.

For instance, if the theme was on Eucharist for a given month, not only would the children of each age group and the adults learn about the meaning of the Mass during the monthly event, they would have activities to do as a family, such as designing a tablecloth similar to ones used on the altar during Mass, or lighting candles during meals, or putting a Bible in a prominent place in the home, or reading about the Eucharist in the bulletin and website, or working out puzzles and coloring pictures in a special edition of the parish newsletter based upon the Eucharist.

When all the various educational committees met to discuss this new intergenerational approach, the commission was delighted with how enthusiastic the leaders were about going in this direction. "Let's do it!" one member of the school board remarked. "For once it would bring the school and religious education programs together. This is what we have been waiting to hear, a creative way to do this."

So positive was the reaction that it moved the staff's timeline up six months. The initial idea of a trial period was left behind. "Let's call it GIFT," a teenager from the youth core team remarked. "It stands for Growing In Faith Together with the emphasis on *together!*" The staff looked at each other wondering whether they could pull it off that soon, but the excitement of the committee members was infectious. "You will all have to pitch in to make this happen," the DRE said with some trepidation. "This has to be a joint effort of us all if we are going to make this transition in such a short time."[31]

Special task groups were arranged on the spot. One was to work out the overall themes and curriculum so that all the basics of the faith would be included over a five- or six-year period. Another focused on publicity and spreading the word so that the entire parish would be eager to attend. A third was to work on the setup of the rooms and on arranging for the meals, while a fourth took charge of designing the take-home materials and the follow-up throughout the month. Members of the adult formation committee volunteered to coordinate the presentations and small group discussions for the adults, while the school board and religious education committee volunteered to work out the details for the breakout sessions involving the various grade levels. The youth core team offered to plan events for the teens during the sessions, as well as have the youth take charge of welcoming people to each of the three weekend sessions.

What followed were months of concentrated efforts by all of the task groups. This was a huge undertaking, changing the way all of religious formation was done in the parish, school included. Religious classes, especially those preparing children for First Communion, Reconciliation, and Confirmation, were changed so that they were conducted as a support and application of the monthly theme rather than a separate entity.

As the first "event" approached, there was an intensive publicity blitz in the parish that including handouts, bulletin inserts, announcements from the pulpit, banners, brochures, emails, website notices — any and everything that would encourage people to attend. The first GIFT weekend was scheduled for the middle of September. The theme was "We Are Family — How to Make It Happen." People could attend any one of the three sessions. The Saturday morning began with a breakfast that the combined Girl Scouts and Boy Scouts agreed to cook. The Sunday session featured a brunch after the last morning Mass, which the Knights of Columbus sponsored, while the Monday evening meal was under the guidance of the Altar and Rosary Society. After the meal, each session began with a common prayer worked out by the formation commission. This was followed by a table activity for all ages and families together. Then came the breakout sessions for each grade level, while the adults remained behind for a talk and small group discussion.

The first "event" was a blazing success. A total of 430 people participated in one or another of the three sessions. The commission's goal was to reach 800 people in a given year. This was well on the way to what initially seemed an impossible number. "We can do it," the youth minister said after the final session. "If the same spirit I saw this last weekend endures, the entire parish will want to attend. I'm not sure where we will put everyone, but it's a nice problem to have."

As the monthly events progressed throughout the year, the numbers attending not only remained stable but kept rising. One of the themes people remembered the most was the focus on Advent, during which the children did a skit on "waiting for the real Christmas, not just for the presents I want to get from Santa Claus." Another was in January where the emphasis was on Martin Luther King's birthday. A special effort was made to welcome all races and ethnic groups in the parish to the event. The monthly take-home activity was to reach out and meet someone beyond one's own heritage and comfort zone. The adult discussion on immigration was talked about in parish circles for many weeks following the weekend presentation.

As the year came to an end the formation commission invited the three staff members back to a Leadership Night. It gave each one a special plaque in appreciation for what had been accomplished in such a short time. No longer were parents dropping off their children for religious education classes; they now came as a family unit and worked on projects together. Both older and younger adults were also attending in large numbers and were discovering new friends in the process. The enthusiasm kept spreading as more and more parishioners discovered the joy of traveling on the faith journey *together*.[32]

Outreach

First-Year Goal: By the year 20___, our parish is connecting with two hundred inactive parishioners, listening to their concerns, and giving them a sense of worth and well-being.

Second-Year Goal: By the year 20___, two-thirds of the parishioners are fully aware of all outreach ministries associated with pastoral care, social service, peace and justice, and connecting with inactive parishioners, and at least a third are taking an active part in these ministries.

Third-Year Goal: By the year 20___ , the parish is providing regular forums for discussing peace and justice issues and is taking active and visible stands on social moral issues based upon Gospel values and church teachings.

◆ ◆ ◆

The outreach commission began with an ambitious goal of connecting with inactive parishioners, that is, those not coming to church any more than once a month, if at all. The attempt was not necessarily getting them back to Mass regularly but rather trying to discover their expectations of church and what was getting in the way of their attendance and involvement in the parish. Why did they stop attending Mass? What were their feelings toward the church at this time? What could the parish do to respond to their issues and concerns?

"Listening," the commission members thought, was the operative word. To accomplish this connecting and listening, a concerted effort would have to be made to find out just who these inactive Catholics were and what kept them on the fringes of parish life. Thankfully the outreach commission had the results from the update of the parish census to get them started. The census committee had made contact with all the parishioners to make sure they were still members of the parish. The committee had also collected any comments and remarks from people as they did the census, both inactive and active alike.[33] With this information in hand, the outreach commission began to formulate its action plan for the coming year.

June: Set up a plan for connecting with at least two hundred of the inactive parishioners and listening to their issues and concerns. Work out a timeline for implementing the plan and a target date for when the tasks are to be completed.

July: Assemble a group of twenty people who agree to connect with ten inactive parishioners each. Name two people as the coordinators and overseers of this group of volunteers.

August: Put together a three-hour training workshop for the volunteers so they are equipped to connect with and listen to the inactive parishioners they contact. This workshop is conducted by qualified presenters who can instruct volunteers on how to listen to people's concerns and issues, how to accept them without criticism or prejudice, and then how to support them without cajoling or trying to get them back to church.

September: Give each of the twenty volunteers ten inactive parishioners to contact during the coming month. The contact begins with a letter signed by the pastor, followed by a phone call from the volunteer and, if possible, a personal visit. If the person shows interest in returning to church, he or she is invited to a "Night of Discovery" to be held during the month of October.

October: Ask staff members and qualified parish ministers to conduct an evening of information about the church and parish. The session would last no more than an hour and a half, including a tour of the church and parish buildings, pausing at significant locations to explain their purpose and significance. One stop, for instance, might be what used to be the confessional but is now the Reconciliation Room. People could gather around the room, sharing stories of their memories of what confession used to be like. The presenters would then explain how the room was used now and the positive role of the sacrament in people's lives. Other stops might include the baptismal font, the sacristy, the parish office, or even the rectory.

November: Offer a second "Night of Discovery" one month later for those who want to hear more about the church and parish or have questions they want answered. For those interested in reconnecting with the parish, a third session is arranged half an hour before one of the weekend liturgies. Each returning parishioner is be paired up with one of the volunteers as a sponsor. The volunteer meets with the person beforehand to offer support and encouragement and then stay with the family or individual throughout the

Mass, offering explanations, when asked, about what was happening. In this way, the less active parishioners have companions to help them on the next step of their faith journey.

January: Assemble the twenty volunteers for a report on their ministry of connecting with and listening to the two hundred inactive members of the parish. These volunteers also have a chance to repeat the exercise during the next five months if they wish; they can also become part of a new committee that would be formed to organize an ongoing outreach process to inactive parishioners.

Once the outreach commission had mapped out its tasks for the next seven or eight months, it went to work locating the twenty volunteers who would help with the project, as well as finding people to lead the Discovery Nights and the follow-up sessions. Rather than forming a committee immediately, the commission members wanted to try out this new process themselves to see if it would do the job and then make needed adjustments before turning it over to a new committee for connecting with inactives.

Once they started the pilot project, the experience of trying to connect with and listen to inactive parishioners was an eye-opener for both the commission itself and the twenty volunteers who made the personal contacts. The reasons that held people back from participating in the parish were as varied as the people who were contacted. For many it was a marriage issue, being in a second marriage and not knowing whether they could still attend church. The volunteers were well trained to listen to the circumstances of each case and then bring these back to the pastor and staff members so that further contact and counsel could be offered. It was a relief to some of the inactive couples to know that their marriages could be blessed with less difficulty, expense, or paperwork than they had anticipated. For others it was falling out of the habit of attending church, often because of a move that disrupted their daily routines and affiliations. This was especially true for the Hispanic parishioners. Still others did not find anything appealing about the Mass they were attending, not knowing there were other parish liturgies that might be more to their liking. "Not knowing" was a common reason for not coming to church. Many people just didn't know what the parish had to offer and how it might speak to their needs and desires. The "Discovery Night" was a turning point for many because it gave them the information they needed to become reacquainted and reconnected with the parish.

As the first year of concentration on inactives drew to a close and a new committee was formed and functioning on its own, the commission turned its attention to its second-year goal. This one centered on visibility, that of making sure that the parishioners were aware of all the outreach ministries that were going on in the parish and understood how they themselves could contribute to and become involved in these ministries.

Unfortunately it was too soon to take advantage of a goal planned by the administration commission. This was the formation of a parish-wide communications committee, which would not be up and running for at least another year. The same was true of the community life commission. It, too, had as a third-year goal the formation of a volunteer coordinating committee. As a result, the outreach commission had to make its own plans for getting the word out about all that was happening in outreach ministries. As the commission began exploring ways to get the word out, it soon discovered that even those involved in these ministries did not know what each of the other groups was doing. No wonder the parishioners were in the dark about these activities if even those working in these areas were ignorant of each other's activities.

What was needed, the commission members concluded, was a two-pronged approach. Start with the ministries themselves, making sure all of them knew what the other groups were doing. Then follow this up with a publicity and marketing effort in the parish that showed off all that was happening.

Each person on the commission had been connecting with the heads of the various outreach ministries each month. Perhaps it was time to call these people together so they could plan a gathering of everyone involved in pastoral care, social service, and peace and justice and connecting with inactive Catholics. Some options included a one-day retreat for all the ministries, or a workshop on caring for people in need, or a show-and-tell session that would give people the chance to tell stories about what they had encountered in ministering to the sick, needy, and inactives.

When the gathering of all the heads of the outreach ministries took place, the commission members explained their goal of making the outreach ministries better known to the parishioners and their plan of having all those involved in these groups come together to get to know one another. Once this had been accomplished, the next step was to get the word out to all the parishioners about what was happening as a means for enlisting their involvement.

As the ministry heads listened to these various options they became excited by what could be accomplished in bringing all their people together. "Let's do it all," one chairperson suggested. "Have a day where there would be time for reflection, followed by some storytelling, mix in a presentation or two, and cap it off with Mass. I'm sure I could get a good turnout from my group."

The idea caught on and by the end of the two-hour meeting, not only was the agenda for the "Retreat and Sharing Day" worked out, but all the duties and tasks needed to make it a success were divided up among the various outreach ministries and groups. A few volunteered to handle the prayer portion of the day, while others took charge of the setup and lunch, and still others agreed to locate one or two presenters or to run the small group sharing and the "Show and Tell" part of the day. The Saturday gathering of all outreach ministers was scheduled for the following month. "It's a bit soon," one commission member cautioned, "but with all this interest and involvement, I think we can pull it off."

And pull it off they did. The ministry heads vied with one another to see who could get the highest percentage of their workers to attend. When the day began, over a hundred people showed up. It was the first time that those taking communion to the sick or those in the bereavement ministry had ever sat down with members of the St. Vincent de Paul Society or those working in the soup kitchen, to say nothing of the peace and justice committee or those involved in pro-life. It was a wonderful depiction of all that the parish was doing to reach out to those in need or to change unjust structures and practices.

First on the agenda was group prayer, followed by individual reflection. This led to random groups of five or six people sharing stories with one another about their intense and sometimes humorous encounters. Next came a talk on how to care for people without trying to solve their problems or be their "savior." People returned to the small groups to discuss how this applied to their own ministering.

After lunch there was a chance to do a "show and tell" about what was happening in all the various outreach ministries. Each group had half an hour to put together a creative presentation about their work, something more than just giving a report, but it had to be done in five minutes or less. The resulting presentations were masterful. Some did role plays or skits. One group offered a PowerPoint presentation on its ministry, while the Haiti Project showed pictures of children they had visited the previous summer.

Before the concluding Mass, the outreach commission asked every group to come up with ideas of how this awareness of each other's ministry could be presented to the parish as a whole. "Do the 'Show and Tell' for the parishioners," was the resounding cry. "Let people in on what we have experienced today," one minister remarked. "We have a goldmine here. Let the parishioners know about this."

And so they did. The outreach commission sponsored a "Show and Tell" town hall meeting after the last Mass on the second Sunday of September. The five best acts from the workshop were chosen for the occasion. All the outreach ministries had tables around the sides of the parish hall with pictures and displays of their activities and events. A massive publicity campaign preceded the town hall meeting, utilizing the one hundred or more outreach ministers who had attended the Retreat and Sharing Day as the marketers and publicists.

As people entered the hall, each was given a sheet that explained all the outreach ministries and a sign-up card for their involvement in one or another of these groups. The co-chairs of the outreach commission who were to do the opening prayer and introductions had to delay the start of the town hall meeting for ten minutes as more and more people poured into the hall and wandered around the perimeter looking at the displays of all that was happening in the various outreach groups and ministries.

The "show and tell" presentations were a great hit, some including music or role plays or pictures. There was even a skit about what it felt like to go through customs in Haiti as members from the parish had to do when they went there for a work camp. The presenters then reversed the situation to include someone from Haiti trying to go through security in an airport in this country. At the end of the town hall meeting, one elderly gentleman remarked, "There is so much going on. I've been here a long time and thought I knew what was happening. Far from it. This is amazing, just amazing."

The town hall meeting was so successful that people asked whether it could become an annual tradition of the parish. The tally of people who signed up for a ministry or wanted someone to contact them numbered fifty-five. The pastor who was standing in the back counting heads made an announcement at the end. "I have never seen such an enthusiastic gathering of people discussing outreach ministries. Most of the time these groups amount to a few dedicated people who work alone and with little fanfare. No more. This crowd of 326 individuals proves it. We are, based on what I have seen today, 'a parish dedicated to the service of others.' I am so proud of everyone who made this possible and for all of you who took the time to attend. Thank you!"

The outreach commission beamed with pride, knowing that this second-year goal had been realized, and then some. At the next

Leadership Night, all of the other commissions congratulated them for a job well done. "This is all fine and good," one of the co-chairs said at the start of their meeting, "but we can't just bask in the glory of what has been accomplished. It is time to look at our third-year goal. This one won't be easy. We have committed ourselves to plan parish forums on peace and justice concerns, which hopefully will lead to the parish taking public stands on social issues. That will be a real challenge. The parish has never done this before. Any ideas how to get started?"

Everyone remained silent until finally one person spoke up. "I have read about something called 'World Café.' It's a new approach to group discussions. People are placed in groups of four around a table to reflect on a pressing issue. After a short time they move to other groups and end up at three or four tables over the course of an evening. Eventually it leads to uncovering ideas about how to move from just talking about an issue to coming up with action plans to deal with it. Maybe we could try out something like that in our parish."

The commission members reacted with relief that at least something surfaced as a way to get started on addressing this challenging goal. "Where can we find out more about this?" a person asked. This led the members to research this concept over the month and to report on all they had learned the next Leadership Night. After everyone shared the results of their research, the co-chair exclaimed, "We can do this! We now have a good process. But what topic should we discuss?"

"How about global warming?" one person suggested. "It is going to be with us for a long time, and people feel so helpless about how to respond to this concern. Maybe this would be a good place to begin. Getting people talking could move us into action." All agreed, and the rest of the evening was devoted to planning the first parish "World Café" process.[34] Based on their reading and research, this is the plan they settled upon:

1. A time is arranged for the process, and parishioners are invited to attend. They are told that only one hundred individuals will be able to attend and that they will have to do some preparation beforehand. This will consist of background reading and watching a film that deals with the issue of global warming. If more than this number respond, then a second session is planned for another evening.

2. Before people arrive, card tables are arranged for four persons each, and the tables are covered with large sheets of blank paper so participants can draw, doodle, or jot down notes on the paper. Markers and crayons are supplied for this purpose.

3. One "host" (or hostess) is trained for each table beforehand. The host remains at the table throughout the process as others move about the room.

4. When people gather, they can choose a table for the first round of discussion. After an initial prayer and explanation of the process, the facilitators announce the first question for discussion: "How did you react to the reading materials and film? What grabbed you or caused you discomfort?" The host at each table makes sure that everyone has a chance to talk ands encourages people to use the paper in any way they wish. The attempt is to tap into both left- and right-brain activity, both thinking and feeling, analysis and synthesis.

5. After fifteen minutes, time is called and everyone, except the table hosts, moves to another table, no two to the same place. When everyone is settled, they share what came out of their first discussion. The facilitators then introduce the new question: "What can each one of us do to help stem the warming trend, and what changes am I willing to make in my own life?"

6. The discussion goes on for fifteen minutes, at the end of which, time is called and everyone chooses a new table. The

host makes notes on the table covering and shares these with the new group, as the rest talk about what they discussed in the last round.

7. The third question for the final fifteen-minute discussion is: "What actions could the parish community take to reverse global warming, and what changes might this mean for the parish as a whole?"

8. At the end of the hour, each table host gives a one-minute report to the large gathering, and the sheets covering the tables are taped to the walls for all to see.

9. After the gathering, the results of the brainstorming are collected and published in the bulletin and put on the parish website. The facilitators also prioritize the suggestions that surfaced and funnel them to the appropriate parish groups and individuals for implementation.

This was the process the commission mapped out for the discussion on global warming. They consulted the pastoral council and other commissions to see what they thought of the idea. All the leadership groups gave them a positive response.

With this encouragement, the commission settled on a date and offered it to the parishioners. Surprisingly the one hundred spots available were filled within a week. A packet of resource materials was given to each person along with a priority list of required readings and suggestions for what more people could do if they had the time. Twenty-five people volunteered to be table hosts, and they met together half an hour before the event.

What happened that evening is lodged in the memories of those who attended. Not only did it open up minds and hearts to the seriousness of the issue; it pushed them into actions and commitments way beyond what any had thought they would be doing when they signed up for the evening.

Administration

First-Year Goal: By the year 20⎯, the parish has an accurate listing of its active and inactive members that is updated on a yearly basis and can be easily accessed for use by staff, leaders, ministers, and parish organizations.

Second-Year Goal: By the year 20⎯, all members of the parish community, both young and old, are strongly encouraged to make stewardship a way of life so that they are giving a proportion of their time in prayer, their talents in service, and their treasure in financial contributions back to God.

Third Year Goal: By the year 20⎯, all parishioners are kept informed about what is happening in the parish through a wide variety of communication vehicles and are given the opportunity to share their opinions and desires with those in leadership positions.

◆ ◆ ◆

The description of how the administration commission translated their first-year goal into action is described in chapter 14. The result was an accurate listing of all parishioners, both active and inactive, in a way that could be easily accessed by staff, leaders, and ministers.

The second-year goal of fostering a stewardship culture in the parish was spelled out in chapter 19, covering the areas of prayer, parish involvement, and financial giving. This leaves the final goal of keeping all the parishioners informed about what is happening in the parish. All of the other commissions were clamoring for the administration commission to get working on this goal as soon as possible. New activities and projects were springing up in many areas of the parish. Up to this time each ministry and group was responsible for its own publicity and advertising. This led to a duplication of efforts, not to mention competition and conflicts among groups.

The administration commission soon realized that its task was not to do the communication but to funnel this responsibility to others and make sure it was being accomplished. The only difficulty was that no such communications group or committee as yet existed in the parish. The first task, therefore, was to make up a job description of what was needed and then find qualified people to form a committee to implement that task.

It was not hard to define the role for this group. Four communication vehicles needed attention. One was the bulletin. At the present moment a part-time secretary put together the bulletin each week, but she only edited whatever people gave her with little thought about how it was being received by the parishioners. Everything seemed to have the same importance, and when taken as a whole, it was not a very attractive vehicle for dispersing information. One of the jobs of the communications committee, therefore, would be to work with the office staff in order to discover ways to make the bulletin a creative and appealing means of communication. It should become something the parishioners would look forward to receiving and reading every week.

Second was the website. It hadn't been kept up-to-date, nor was it interactive enough. Much more could happen with the parish website, especially as a connection with younger adults who tended to use this medium to a greater extent than the older people. This was a critical service a new communications committee might offer the parish. The website could be an exciting link to the parish community, full of interesting tidbits about all that was happening. It might also include easy-to-use links to parish groups and ministries so that people could learn more about them and even sign up to volunteer their time and services online. The possibilities become limitless once the website is used to its full potential.

The communications committee could also resurrect the newsletter. It had fallen into disuse over the last few years, and nothing had been done to bring it back to life. The communications committee could make up a new format that was filled with pictures and stories about events and activities taking place in the parish. It would be a complement to the bulletin and website as a valuable source of information. All parish groups, ministries, and organizations could be recognized and receive accolades for their work and achievements. Creating a newsletter four, six, or eight times a year, the commission realized, would be no easy task. But with the right balance of reporters, photographers, editors, and layout experts, the result would be well worth the effort. It wouldn't have to be slick or fancy, just full of pictures of people enjoying themselves, along with stories about children, teens, families, singles, and the elderly.[35]

The final aspect of the communications committee's role would be to create an inviting and welcoming atmosphere around the parish. This might include signs and banners, pictures and handouts, brochures and logos — anything that could publicize the spirit and energy of the parish. As the administration commission envisioned this aspect of the committee's task, the members became excited about the possibilities, such as large signs describing where each building and meeting room was located, banners on the light posts coming up the road toward the church, huge pictures of children and families in the gathering area, attractive brochures detailing parish events, posters and bulletin boards, even streamers and flags on the walls both inside and out. "The place would be flooded with good news about the parish," one commission member exclaimed. "No one could be a member of this place without knowing all that is happening."

After determining what the job would entail, the next step was to locate likely people for staffing the committee. "Our parish must be filled with people who have skills in graphic arts, publicity, marketing, and communications," one person remarked. "The trick will be to find these people and invite them to contribute their expertise and experience to the parish community. I suspect that many of them will feel privileged to be asked to join this most important group."

To get started, the commission members spent the month asking the staff and other commissions to suggest names of people to chair this committee. Those suggested had to be good leaders who could motivate others. Once they narrowed down the field, they personally invited two likely candidates to the next Leadership Night. At the meeting they spelled out the duties and tasks of the new communications committee. After the two people — somewhat overwhelmed — heard what was being asked of them, they asked for a few days to think it over. Within a week they both said yes, although they admitted they didn't know where to begin or where to find recruits for this committee. The commission members were delighted with the new co-chairs' willingness to give it a try and eased their concerns somewhat by giving them the names of all the others who were known to have expertise and experience in this area. The commission also gave the co-chairs a description of the committee's task, a timeline for implementation, and a request for progress reports over the next six to ten months.

The implementation of the commission's third-year goal was now in the hands of the newly formed communications committee. All the commission members could do now was step back and let the committee do the rest.

To get started, the committee of twelve split into four small task groups, three members each. One concentrated on the bulletin, spending time with the office secretary to offer her ideas about reformatting and layout. She was appreciative to have others work with her on this because she had been doing the bulletin with little or no help or direction. Within a month the bulletin was reorganized under five headings that corresponded to the five commissions. Parishioners could now easily locate information associated with worship, community life, formation, outreach, and administration. The change in appearance was striking, and the parishioners responded accordingly. "I know where to look for what is happening in my area," a liturgical minister declared. "It's so much easier to use, and the calendar of parish happenings that comes out as an insert each month is posted on my refrigerator so I can keep track of everything going on, something I could never do before."

The new website became the talk of the parish. Not only did it have sections for each of the commission areas, but people could sign up for ministries online, as well as get schedules of meetings and parish events, give feedback about everything that is going on in the parish, even provide feedback about the homilies. Each of the events taking place in the parish had pictures posted on the website. This got people interested in taking a look to see if their own family was included. The three committee members who headed up this task force kept asking each other, "Why has the parish waited so long to do this? It's not that hard a task, and it goes so far in keeping people plugged into parish happenings and projects."

The bimonthly newsletter was also becoming a hit. A group of photographers began attending every parish event. Even the pastor got into the act as a way of testing out his new digital camera. Sending pictures via email to the three editors made it easy for them to meet deadlines. Each issue had its own theme, beginning with the goals and action plans of the commissions for the coming year, one commission per issue. Commission members vied with one another to make their issue the most appealing. "I know we are not into competition here," one commission member reported, "but you have to admit that having the newsletter concentrate on what we have accomplished brings out the best in each of our commissions." Parishioners had the choice of receiving the newsletter through the mail as a hardcopy or via email. Some asked for it both ways so they would make sure to see it.

Finally, the three people working on "image building" in the parish had the furthest to go and eventually the most to show for their efforts. Not much had been done to make the parish accessible to strangers and newcomers who came to the parish. The parishioners took for granted that people would know where to go for what meetings or to gain assistance. This was not the case for those unfamiliar with the parish campus. As proof of this, one member of the communications committee brought an old friend from out of town to the parish and asked him what he experienced in first encountering the parish. "I don't know where to go," was the reaction. "Even the office is not that easy to locate, and to find where to go for a meeting is beyond me."

"Just as I suspected," the committee member responded. With this information in hand, along with many other similar examples, the task group of three initiated an ambitious project of "putting the parish on the map." They were able to obtain some funds from the finance council to construct signs and permanent maps of the campus, as well as informative brochures and handouts about the parish. They made proofs of all of these materials and circulated them among the staff and commissions for reactions and suggestions. Once this was accomplished, the new signs and brochures began appearing one month at a time so parishioners would have a chance to react and give their feedback. The response was very positive. "It's about time we made ourselves known around here," the head of the women's club remarked. "All the other churches around here make it easy for people to discover where they are located and what they offer. Not us. It's always been a big secret. Time for us to do a little showing off, I say."

This comment made the pastor laugh, but he had to acknowledge that the image of the parish needed some attention. "Whatever we are doing as a parish makes no difference if people don't know where we are. With this new emphasis on publicity and image-building, the word is getting out in new and wonderful ways. Since we began this shift away from me and the staff doing everything to the formation of commissions and new committees, this place has taken off. I could never have dreamed that so much could be accomplished in such a short time. All that was required was for me to give it a blessing and then get out of the way. This new communications committee is a case in point."

"I beg to differ," the parish administrator remonstrated. "You did far more than bless it and get out of the way. You gave it legitimacy — the whole thing, from staff to council to commissions to committees. You stayed with it so that everyone else kept up their side of the bargain and did what they said they would do. You were willing to enter into partnership with me. You kept my feet to the fire, along with everyone else's. You saw what could happen and then got the rest of us to join you in this adventure. Now the parish belongs to all of us — and just try to tell us differently. Look what God has done for us! We are one blessed, faith-filled community, and your style of leadership has had much to do with this coming about. Thank you."

Notes

1. St. Paul: Star Thrower Distribution, *www.starthrower.com.*
2. Ibid.
3. This statement, although it has been significantly changed, was inspired by Michael W. Foss, *Power Surge* (Minneapolis: Fortress Press, 2000).
4. Thomas Sweetser, S.J., *The Parish as Covenant: A Call to Pastoral Partnership* (Lanham, MD: Sheed and Ward, 2001).
5. Two resources are Stephen's Ministry (*www.stephenministry.org*) and BeFriender Ministry (*www.befrienderministry.org*).
6. The worship commission will be discussed in chapter 8, and the liturgy planning committee in the "Worship" section of the appendix.
7. See Carol Holden, Thomas Sweetser, and Mary Beth Vogel, *Recreating the Parish* (Lanham, MD: Sheed and Ward, 1996).
8. See chapter 10 for a further explanation of these areas.
9. A sample copy of the covenant booklet can be obtained from the Parish Evaluation Project, 3195 South Superior Street, Milwaukee, WI 54207, 414-483-7370, *www.pepparish.org.*
10. The process for decision making will be treated at length in chapter 18.
11. My thanks to Our Lady of the Assumption parish in Claremont, California, and to Padre Serra parish in Camarillo, California, for sharing their nomination process and their method of selection of new commission members.
12. A sample survey for the weekend liturgies is provided later in this chapter.
13. Contact the Parish Evaluation Project for information about surveying and information gathering, 414-483-7370.
14. See Patricia Forster, O.S.F., and Thomas Sweetser, S.J.,*Transforming the Parish: Models for the Future,* 2nd ed. (Lanham, MD: Sheed and Ward, 1999), 99–101.

15. See the *Seminary Journal* (Winter 2005) book review section, 89–91, as well as Michael Papesh, *Clerical Culture: Contradiction and Transformation* (Collegeville, MN: Liturgical Press, 2004.)

16. See chapter 18 for an explanation of the C-D-I of decision making.

17. Adapted from J. B. Phillips translation.

18. Contact: *www.dioceseofsaginaw.org* or telephone 989-799-7910.

19. See the Appendix under the Community Life section (pages 226ff.) for a description of the volunteer coordinating committee.

20. See Thomas P. Sweetser, S.J., and Mary Benet McKinney, O.S.B., *Changing Pastors: A Resource for Pastoral Transitions* (Lanham, MD: Sheed and Ward, 1998).

21. See chapter 11, as well as Forster and Sweetser, *Transforming the Parish*, 99–101, for more on the process of large group discernment.

22. Richard McBrien, *Catholicism* (Minneapolis: Winston Press, 1980), 1057.

23. Ibid., 252.

24. "A Quest for the Holy," Religious Education Congress, in Anaheim, California, 2004.

25. See Most Holy Redeemer Parish in San Francisco, 415-863-6259, *www.mhr.org.*

26. St. Patrick's Parish, 312-648-1021, *www.oldstpats.org.*

27. St. Monica's Parish, 310-393-9287, *www.stmonica.net.*

28. Robert Wuthnow, *All In Sync* (Berkeley: University of California Press, 2003), 146.

29. St. Mary's Parish, 316-788-5525, *www.stmarysderby.com.*

30. Ronald Rolheiser, O.M.I., *The Holy Longing* (New York: Doubleday, 1999), 134–40.

31. See Our Lady of Lourdes Parish in Milwaukee, WI, from whom the acronym GIFT is borrowed. 414-545-4316, *www.olol.4lpi.com.*

32. For more information about this approach to intergenerational learning, see Whole Community Catechesis (*www.twentythirdpublications.com*) and the Generations of Faith Project (*www.cmdnet.org*), as well as the writings of Bill Huebsch and John Roberto.

33. See chapter 14 for a description of the census committee's work in response to the administration commission's first-year goal.

34. See Juanita Brown, with David Isaacs, *World Café* (San Francisco: Berrett-Koehler Publishers, 2005). Also *www.theworldcafe.com.*

35. See St. Mary's Parish in Derby, Kansas, for an example of an attractive parish newsletter. 316-788-5525, *www.stmarysderby.com.*

Selected Readings

Becker, Carol E. *Becoming Colleagues: Women and Men Serving Together in Faith.* San Francisco: Jossey-Bass, 2000.

Brown, Juanita, with David Isaacs. *World Café.* San Francisco: Berrett-Koehler Publishers, 2005.

Clark, William A., S.J. *A Voice of Their Own: The Authority of the Local Parish.* Collegeville, MN: Liturgical Press, 2005.

Cuzzons, Donald B. *Faith That Dares to Speak.* Collegeville, MN: Liturgical Press, 2004.

———. *Freeing Celibacy.* Collegeville, MN: Liturgical Press, 2006.

D'Antonio, William V., James D. Davidson, Dean R. Hoge, and Katherine Meyer. *American Catholics: Gender, Generation and Commitment.* Walnut Creek, CA: Alta Mira Press, 2001.

Fiand, Barbara S.N.D.deN. *A Quest for the Holy.* Anaheim, CA: Religious Education Congress, 2004.

Froehle, Bryan T., and Mary L. Gautier. *Catholicism USA: A Portrait of the Catholic Church in the United States.* Maryknoll, NY: Orbis Books, 2000.

Forster, Patricia, O.S.F., and Thomas Sweetser, S.J. *Transforming the Parish: Models for the Future.* 2nd ed. Lanham, MD: Sheed and Ward, 1999.

Foss, Michael W. *Power Surge.* Minneapolis: Fortress Press, 2000.

Gull, Thomas. *The Complete Parish.* Schillar Park, IL: J. S. Paluch Press, 2003.

Hater, Robert J. *The Catholic Parish: Hope in a Changing World.* Mahwah, NJ: Paulist Press, 2004.

Hendricks, Kathy. *Everything about Parish Ministry I Wish I Had Known.* Mystic, CT: Twenty-Third Publications, 2002.

Hiesberger, Jean Marie. *Fostering Leadership Skills in Ministry.* Liguori, MO: Liguori Publishers, 2002.

Hoge, Dean R. *The First Five Years of the Priesthood.* Collegeville, MN: Liturgical Press, 2002.

———. *Experiences of Priests Ordained Five to Nine Years.* Washington, DC: National Catholic Education Association, 2006.

Hoge, Dean, and Jacqueline Wenger. *Evolving Visions of the Priesthood: Changes from Vatican II to the Turn of the Century.* Collegeville, MN: Liturgical Press, 2003.

Holden, Carol, Thomas Sweetser, and Mary Beth Vogel. *Recreating the Parish: Reproducible Resources for Pastoral Ministers.* Lanham, MD: Sheed and Ward, 1996.

Huebsch, Bill. *Whole Community Catechesis.* Mystic, CT: Twenty-Third Publications, 2002, 2003.

Jeselson, Mary Ann, ed. *Great Ideas from Great Parishes.* Liguori, MO: Liguori Publishers, 2002.

Johnson, Elizabeth A. *The Church Women Want.* New York: Herder and Herder, 2002.

Lakeland, Paul, *The Liberation of the Laity.* New York: Continuum Press, 2002.

Law, Eric H. F. *The Bush Was Blazing but Not Consumed.* St. Louis: Chalice Press, 1996.

———. *Inclusion: Making Room for Grace.* St. Louis: Chalice Press, 2000.

———. *Sacred Acts, Holy Change, Faithful Diversity and Practical Transformation.* St. Louis: Chalice Press, 2002.

———. *The Wolf Shall Dwell with the Lamb: A Spirituality for Leadership in a Multicultural Community.* St. Louis: Chalice Press, 1993.

Lowney, Chris. *Heroic Leadership.* Chicago: Loyola Press, 2003.

McBrien, Richard. *Catholicism.* Minneapolis: Winston Press, 1980.

Oakley, Francis, and Bruce Russett, eds. *Governance, Accountability and the Future of the Catholic Church.* New York: Continuum Press, 2004.

Papesh, Michael L. *Clerical Culture: Contradiction and Transformation.* Collegeville, MN: Liturgical Press, 2004.

Parish Evaluation Project. *Parish Assessment and Renewal: A Process for Parish Strategic Planning.* 3195 S. Superior Street, Milwaukee, WI, 414-483-7370.

Rivers, Robert S. C.S.P. *From Maintenance to Mission: Evangelization and the Revitalization of the Parish.* Mahwah, NJ: Paulist Press, 2005.

Rolheiser, Ronald. *The Holy Longing: The Search for a Christian Spirituality.* New York: Doubleday, 1999.

Schoenherr, Richard. *Goodbye Father: Celibacy and Patriarchy in the Catholic Church.* Ed. David A. Yamane. New York: Oxford University Press, 2003.

Schuth, Katarina. *Priestly Ministry in Multiple Parishes.* Collegeville, MN: Liturgical Press, 2006.

Smith, Christian. *Soul Searching: The Religious and Spiritual Lives of American Teenagers.* New York: Oxford University Press, 2005.

Sofield, Loughlan, and Carroll Juliano. *Collaboration: Uniting Our Gifts in Ministry.* Notre Dame, IN: Ave Maria Press, 2000.

Stillwell, Virginia. *Priestless Parishes: The Baptized Leading the Baptized.* Allen, TX: Thomas More, 2002.

Sweetser, Thomas P., S.J. Book Review of *Clerical Culture: Contradiction and Transformation*. *Seminary Journal* (Winter 2005): 89–91.

———. *The Parish as Covenant: A Call to Pastoral Partnership*. Lanham, MD: Sheed and Ward, 2001.

Sweetser, Thomas P., S.J., and Mary Benet McKinney, O.S.B. *Changing Pastors: A Resource for Pastoral Transitions*. Lanham, MD: Sheed and Ward Publishers, 1998.

Untener, Bishop Ken. *The Practical Prophet: Pastoral Writings*. Mahwah, NJ: Paulist Press, 2007.

———. *Preaching Better: Practical Suggestions for Homilies*. Mahwah, NJ: Paulist Press, 1999.

Wallace, Ruth A. *They Call Him Pastor: Married Men in Charge of Catholic Parishes*. Mahwah, NJ: Paulist Press, 2003.

Wilkes, Paul. *Excellent Catholic Parishes: A Guide to Best Places and Practices*. Mahwah, NJ: Paulist Press, 2001.

Wood, Susan K., ed. *Ordering the Baptismal Priesthood*. Collegeville, MN: Liturgical Press, 2003.

Wuthnow, Robert. *All in Sync*. Berkeley: University of California Press, 2003.

Index

Of Related Interest

John J. Dietzen
CATHOLIC Q & A
All You Want to Know about Catholicism

NEWLY EXPANDED AND UPDATED

Real Questions by Real People

This award-winning popular book offers candid information and engaging advice that speaks to every Catholic and everyone curious about Catholicism. It's all here: answers about matters of the practice of faith; personal morality; Catholic traditions or interpretation of Scripture. Authoritative, readable, intuitively organized with a clear, well-defined index.

Father John J. Dietzen, a parish priest from Peoria, Illinois, has answered questions for decades, drawing on his own expertise and the knowledge of authorities around the world.

ISBN 978-8245-2600-9, paper

Of Related Interest

Ronald Rolheiser
AGAINST AN INFINITE HORIZON
The Finger of God in Our Everyday Lives

Full of personal anecdotes, healing wisdom, and a fresh reflection on Scripture, *Against an Infinite Horizon* draws on the great traditions of parable and storytelling. In this prequel to the bestseller *The Holy Longing*, Rolheiser's new fans will be delighted with further insights into social justice, community, sexuality, mortality, and rediscovering the deep beauty and poetry of Christian spirituality.

"Ronald Rolheiser has mastered the old, old art of parable." — Morris West

"A felicitous blend of scriptural reflection, shrewd psychological observations, and generous portions of letters sent to Rolheiser and his responses." — *Commonweal*

0-8245-1965-5, $16.95, paperback

Of Related Interest

Ronald Rolheiser
THE SHATTERED LANTERN
Rediscovering a Felt Presence of God

The way back to a lively faith "is not a question of find-ing the right answers, but of living a certain way. The existence of God, like the air we breathe, need not be proven...." Rolheiser shines new light on the contem-plative path of Western Christianity and offers a dynamic way forward.

"Whenever I see Ron Rolheiser's name on a book, I know that it will be an amazing combination of true orthodoxy and revolutionary insight — and written in a clear and readable style. He knows the spiritual terrain like few others, and you will be profoundly illuminated by this lantern. Read and be astonished."
— *Richard Rohr, O.F.M.,*
Center for Action and Contemplation,
Albuquerque, New Mexico

0-8245-1884-5, paperback

Check your local bookstore for availability.
To order directly from the publisher,
please call 1-800-888-4741 for Customer Service
or visit our Web site at *www.CrossroadPublishing.com.*
For catalog orders, please send your request to the address below.

info@CrossroadPublishing.com

crossroad